The Hathor Material
Messages from an Ascended Civilization

The Hathor photograph by Gregg Braden.

This photographic image is from a newly discovered temple complex in Memphis, Egypt. Covered with sand and silt from ancient Nile floods, this temple sculpture is particularly significant as it contains the best preserved representation of the Hathors to date. Original photograph of the sculpture by Gregg Braden, 1987.

The Hathor Material
Messages from an Ascended Civilization

Tom Kenyon
and
Virginia Essene

 S.E.E. Publishing Company, Santa Clara, California, USA

This book is manufactured in the United States of America.

Printed on recycled paper.

Hathor Photograph: Gregg Braden
Cover Design: Garret Moore

ISBN # 0-937147-10-9
Library of Congress Catalog Card Number: 96-92424

Second Printing December 1997

Spiritual Education Endeavors
Publishing Company
1556 Halford Avenue, #288
Santa Clara, CA 95051-2661
USA
Tel. (408) 245-5457

Dedication

Dedication from Tom

I dedicate this book to the One, to the One life that lives through all forms, to the One who breathes the breath of all creatures, and to the One Heart of universal love that unites all things. May we awaken to its call and to the sanctity of life. May we learn to give the gifts of compassion to ourselves and to each other.

Tom Kenyon
Birch Bay, Washington
May 17, 1996

Dedication from Virginia

This book is dedicated to our Creator, whatever its many names may be, to the beloved spiritual guides of all dimensions, times, and places who patiently lead us back to Divine consciousness, and to all life forms everywhere who positively contribute to the expansion of life, love, and wisdom.

I also wish to honor my fellow sisters and brothers of planet Earth who share with me a common heritage and an ever-expanding cosmic journey.

Virginia Essene
Santa Clara, California
May 23, 1996

Acknowledgments
by Tom and Virginia

Many helping hearts and hands have served in transcribing the innumerable audio tapes of Tom and Virginia speaking with the Hathors, onto hard copy, as a step in the editing and publishing process. For their loving acts of transcription, and their many hours of volunteer labor, we especially acknowledge Carlos Haylock, Patricia Barrantine, Lynda Keith, Barbara Sawicki, Sherry Bender, Janice Samuelson, Patricia Seek, and Briana Rose.

We also wish to thank Paula Savage who suggested ideas for the diagrams included in the book, and thanks to Garret Moore who completed them.

Special gratitude also goes to the vision and commitment of the SHARE Foundation Board...to Pat Proud for her thoughtful editorial assistance...to Ron Cantoni, for his book design and desktop publishing efforts...to staff member Jan Riqueros for shifting assignments as needed...and to office manager Alma Scheer for her invaluable support throughout the publishing project.

Then let Tom's and Virginia's Earthly gratitude be clearly acknowledged here, along with that of the Hathor's who have also frequently registered their own appreciation to all members of the "Earth team" for our committed efforts. In ways difficult to describe, this book's publication is the demonstration of a cooperative act of spiritual group consciousness on many levels and dimensions!

Thanks to one and all!!

Introduction
by Tom

**"Minds are like parachutes.
They only work when open."**

The material you are about to read comes from a most unusual source—a group of interdimensional beings known collectively as the Hathors. These beings claim to exist in the fourth dimension of our Universe. They are our elder brothers and sisters in consciousness, and they have been involved with mankind for millennia. In ancient Egypt they worked through the fertility cult of the sky goddess, *Hator*. They are masters of sound and energy.

A little over three years ago I was unexpectedly approached by one of these beings during meditation. At that time I was given detailed instruction in a system of sacred geometry designed to open the higher brain centers called ICT or Interdimensional Consciousness Training. According to the Hathors, we have 3,200 *chakras* in the brain, the *ajna* or third eye and crown *chakras* being only two in the head.

This book has come into existence because the Hathors requested it. I certainly had no desire to write such a thing myself. I was very busy with my psychotherapeutic practice, research, and teaching. For the previous two years or so I had been teaching the ICT work throughout the United States with wonderful results. It was very clear to me that this "inner technology" was changing people's lives for the better.

I had also been doing sound work with the Hathors

which was most intriguing since much of my background is in the area of psychoacoustics (the study of how sound, language and music affect consciousness). Most of my "Hathor group's" work is done through the use of sound, specifically via toning in which I align with my mentors and allow them to make sounds through my voice. This work was fascinating for me and often powerful for those experiencing it. I had integrated this part of their work and was fairly comfortable with it when my "Hathor group" asked me to "channel" a book for those who were not able to hear their sounds in person. I balked at the idea. I did not see myself as a "channel" (although I think in some ways we are all channels), and I did not want to get involved with such an undertaking. After a good deal of coaxing on their part, however, I relented and agreed to write their book.

I found that I could not bring their thoughts through in written form at the computer since my internal "editor" would come in and want to change punctuation and grammar mid-stream, which threw me out of the trance state. Since I did not have enough time to record the information onto tape and then transcribe it, I basically told the Hathors to forget it and find someone else. I certainly had no pretense that I was the only "channel" for this information. And so I forgot it, and so had the Hathors, or so I thought.

About four months later, the Hathors shocked me and got my full and rapt attention while I was visiting the San Francisco Bay area. I was giving an introductory evening event before a weekend Hathor workshop when a woman came up to me in the line of people asking questions. She introduced herself as Virginia Essene. I knew the name since I had read some of her books but we had never met before.

You need to realize, too, that there was only one person who knew about the thwarted book attempt, my wife Pam. So here this complete stranger comes up to me and says "Hi...my name is Virginia Essene and I feel a little odd about conveying a message for you since we haven't met yet, but I have one for you."

I remember saying to go ahead.

She then told me that her guidance and the Hathors had come and asked her help to get me to realize the importance of this book. I was dumbfounded. For a moment I couldn't speak and then I laughed. What a hoot!

I told Virginia that I had, in fact, tried to write the material down but I was too busy to transcribe anything. Without missing a beat, Virginia volunteered her publishing group to help in the project and so the Hathors found a willing midwife through Virginia and the SHARE Foundation. Without them this book would not have been written. And so I wish to thank Virginia for her openness and vision. I wish to thank her and her staff for their help in the myriad details involved in such a project. And I also wish to thank those who helped transcribe this taped material onto printed format for Virginia's editing.

The Hathors have said repeatedly that our human feelings are an important aspect of conscious evolution. And so I would ask you to sense your own feeling responses to their words and to their ideas. Don't just accept them as intellectual concepts, but rather sense how they reverberate in your own heart and mind. The Hathors are truly some of the most loving and masterful beings I have yet encountered, and it is an honor for me to be able to introduce you to these most ancient of sages. I trust that you will be touched as deeply by them as I have been.

Open those parachutes!

Tom Kenyon
Washington State
January 12, 1996
(On this day, Uranus enters Aquarius)

Introduction
by Virginia

Over the past 10 years, the SHARE Foundation, via its S.E.E. Publishing Company, has brought you 6 books–and now this 7th publication–representing a wide variety of channeled information. Our purpose has been to challenge your present perceptions, open up unused portions of your true nature, and to inspire your continuing spiritual awakening–your mental, physical and emotional growth and health.

Because many other people and organizations have done something similar during this past decade, particularly, for which I am eternally grateful, the concept of inter-dimensional telepathic communication is becoming more acceptable than ever before. Certainly as we approach the year 2,000 A.D. and become increasingly familiar with our local solar system, and the existence of other areas far beyond, I believe many ancient cellular memories have now been stirred in our unconscious. Indeed, this cellular expansion has opened up our interest in the many ancient mysteries that can now be shared...and in the many healing practices that prior positive civilizations are revealing.

We are learning that life is not random and that the observer and the observed are part of the same circle. If this is fact, not fiction, then our human family is both creating and witnessing its very own transformation, and we can use all the help we can get for this evolutionary advancement!

It gives me great joy, therefore, to introduce the Hathors, presently in the etheric levels of planet Venus, who were formerly very influential in Earth history. This ascended civilization has incredible abilities in the use of sound for healing, which they now come to share with us through the cooperation of Tom Kenyon. From personal experience with Tom in his various seminars, I believe the Hathors' information and energy processes are very powerful and positive. Nonetheless, only you can determine the value of their message for you.

Because Tom has a four and one-half octave vocal range when he tones or chants using the Hathor energy, the sounds are incredible, really quite "other worldly" and extraordinary. So I recommend that you experience him in person, if possible, or at the least that you buy his tapes—especially the one he has prepared to accompany the exercises in this book.

The way in which the Hathors have chosen to communicate their message to planet Earth brings both information and practical energy techniques. In our book they present their comments in the first part of each chapter, followed by answers to my own questions that are intended to clarify or expand their material. Obviously, I couldn't ask every question I had, because of space limitations, nor could my questions include everything you might have wanted to ask, but I hope they will be useful.

Now then, we joyfully present this first printed contact by the Hathors for your own growth and inspiration...and for the highest and best good for the planet and life everywhere.

Peace, dear friends, and blessings on us all!

Virginia Essene

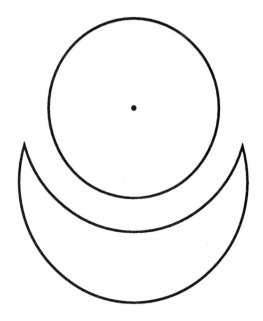

The ancient alchemical symbol above denotes the "sacred mystical" marriage of the masculine and feminine. This "marriage" is not a secular event.

Rather it is something that occurs deep within the individual human, a balancing of one's own internal life forces. As an individual balances the so-called masculine and feminine "currents," one enters a state known as the "universal androgyne." This balanced state of consciousness opens the portal to the deeper mysteries of one's own consciousness.

The round disk signifies the "Sun" or positively charged electrical force. The crescent at the bottom signifies the "Moon" or negatively charged magnetic force. The balancing of electrical and magnetic forces within one's own being is one of the goals of Egyptian Alchemy.

We have placed this symbol in this book as a kind of silent prayer. It is our fervent desire that the battle between man and woman, whether in the outer world or the inner, come to a close—that the peace of balance be found by all persons within the sacred temples of their own hearts—and that this peace "that passeth all understanding" be spread throughout the world.

Contents

Chapter 1
Who We Are and Why We Have Come

We are the Hathors. We come in love and with the sounding of a new dream reality for your Earth. If you are ready to build the new world, we invite you to join us on a journey of the mind and heart. We are your elder brothers and sisters. We have been with you for a very long period of your evolution on this planet. We were with you in eons past–even in the forgotten days before any trace of us is known in your present written history. Our own nature is energetic and interdimensional. We originally came from another universe by way of Sirius which is a portal to your Universe, and from Sirius we eventually proceeded to your solar system and the etheric realms of Venus.

In the past we have specifically worked with and through the *Hator* fertility goddess of ancient Egypt. (Editor's note: For the sake of clarity, we will use the spelling "*Hator*" exclusively for the Egyptian goddess and the spelling "Hathor" for those ascended beings referred to in this book.) We also made contact with the Tibetan lamas in the formative period of Tibetan Buddhism. Thus, some of their unique techniques and practices about the use of sound come from our own lineage and our teachings with them. Although we have interacted with some of Earth's early cultures, we are an intergalactic civilization with outposts that span parts of your known Universe and beyond.

We are what you might term an ascended civilization–a group of beings existing at a specific vibratory field,

1

even as you have an energy signature. It is simply that we vibrate at a faster rate than you. Nonetheless, we are all part of the mystery, part of the love that holds and binds all the universes together.

We have grown as you have grown, ascending to the One Source of all that is. We have grown in joy and through sorrow, as have you. We are, in terms of the vastness, a little higher on the spiral of awareness and consciousness than you are; therefore, we can offer you what we have learned, as friends, mentors and fellow travelers on the path that leads back to remembrance of All That Is.

We are in a great period of healing at all levels of this local solar system and in all kingdoms—not just human. And yet, you humans hold a key for the evolution and the ascension of your planet Earth. That key requires free will choice, and what you humans choose, or do not choose, affects many kingdoms in this world. You are poised at a momentous time in the history of consciousness on this planet. Something is occurring that has never occurred before, and it is a joy and a kind of ecstasy for us to participate with you once again and to come into your conscious awareness. For the last time we were together consciously was in ancient Egypt.

Egyptian history holds few clues to our existence, our motives, or our physical description. However, there are carvings left behind from the temples of *Hator* that show our likeness. A photograph of one such carving appears twice in this book and may serve as a remembrance for some of you.

In the pages that follow we will attempt to bring to you tools and understanding from our level of awareness. It is our hope and our desire that these will prove helpful to you. We want to be clear that we are not your saviors. We are not messianic. We are your brothers and your sisters who dwell close to you, yet we will not intrude in your choice-making nor into your evolution, for that is your own free will.

But we do stand ready to assist you. We stand ready to assist you, not just through the techniques and the understanding that we will reveal in these pages, but we are ready to work with you intimately and individually for greater health and consciousness. Your choosing this book is a sign of willingness, and we are ready and available to you on many levels of consciousness. By offering our aid, however, we do not wish to interfere with your other spiritual helpers and cosmic relationships in any way, nor with any religious beliefs, affiliations or organizations of help to you. Even so, there is a great deal we would like to share.

Then let us begin with an understanding of yourself as energy. Energy is where we will begin our comments because, upon the Earth at this time, consciousness is locked and fixated on what you would call three-dimensional reality–the material world that you can touch and see with your physical senses. And yet, within the spectrum of energies, the electromagnetic spectrum that your physicists have uncovered, *you can only see less than one percent of what exists!* We exist in that other *99 percent* of unperceived energy as do the innumerable other kingdoms of this Universe you have yet to identify.

If you but understood how cherished you are in the other realms, you would be able to release the shackles of self-abnegation that have held your species for centuries. Yet thankfully, all of that is beginning to be erased–which brings us great joy and laughter. Indeed, you will find that we elder brothers and sisters have a sense of humor because the manifestation of the One Source unfolding into infinite realms and levels is essentially joyful, even humorous. For it is a joke, is it not, that the infinite can place itself in the finite? It's like taking the sky and putting it into a glass jar thinking all the while that you are the glass jar–until one day the glass jar shatters and the sky is freed. Don't be afraid of the shattering, friends. It does not need to be difficult. It does not need to be sorrowful. It can be joyful. Happy. And very, very comical.

With these comments, it is now our recommendation that you bring forth any questions that may have arisen. Do you have specific questions you wish to ask, Virginia?

Virginia: Since I want to introduce you Hathors in a way that will help people feel a sense of intimacy, please describe how many are in the group or council that are working to bring us this information. And please give any identifying factors about your interests or areas of expertise in different fields. We'd like to get that information in this first chapter so people can have a sense of meeting you, as it were.

Hathors: We are a group of ten. There are actually thirteen of us but three are not involved in the transmission of this material. They are witnesses and stand back from this process. The ten of us are expressing more or less as a group consciousness, and are being channeled primarily through one of our group, whose name is Avar.

Virginia: Avar?

Hathors: Yes. We are ten individuals out of a civilization of several million. Our background includes what you would call a physician, a scientist, several teachers and historians. There is one of us who is also what you might term a mystic or philosopher, although by nature we are all mystical and philosophical. So, in our group, we have very different and varying perspectives.

Virginia: You obviously chose to do this. Can you give us the reason why?

Hathors: We cherish and love our human brothers and sisters. We sense and we see a tremendous change unfolding on this planet. You are in the midst of a birthing process into a new dimension of consciousness. Our civilization has been through this process, as well. We know intimately the birthing pains of passing through the portal of time and space into a greater reality. Therefore, out of our love and compassion and our joy to be with humans, we have chosen to bring forth this material in hopes that it will assist you.

Virginia: Well, we certainly thank you for that! Can you clarify for us this aspect of the feminine principle—this feminine, creative, fertile quality that the name Hathor seems to imply?

Hathors: Yes. Everything in the Universe is cyclic in nature and dualistic in nature until you get to the fundamental octave that integrates all duality in unity. But all things in the Universe—the physical Universe and all the other subtle universes—have polarity. In terms of human metaphors, these polarities are masculine and feminine or positive and negative electrical charges.

At the time of our coming to the early consciousness of mankind, your emerging consciousness was in touch with the Great Earth which you might call the Great Mother. The great religions of the past did refer to Earth as the Great Mother. And so it was that early consciousness here was deeply connected to this Earth matrix, this consciousness of Earth as feminine, so the feminine mysteries and the feminine nature were the fundamental expressions of consciousness. Then, as the feminine began to be overtaken by what would be termed the masculine, we as your witnesses observed certain things occurring. Humans began a disconnection from Earth and a movement into autonomy. While it is important that mankind come to a realization of its autonomy, being disconnected from the Earth and from the interconnectedness of all life, is very dangerous. What is now happening is that human consciousness is beginning to sense that it must return to the honoring of the Great Mother Earth. And this is a cyclic progression.

In the early formative period of Egyptian cosmology, the goddess *Hator* was associated with the sky. (It was later that *Hator* became identified as the fertility goddess.) It is no accident that her name and ours are similar. We seeded and assisted this early symbol of the feminine

5

mystery. The goddess *Hator* does have an independent existence separate from us and she is, what might be termed, an "archetypal pattern." She is a cosmic force that can be metaphorized, and we, as a culture, have identified with her qualities of love, ecstasy and bliss.

Presently, human consciousness has gone through two polarities–the Earth consciousness of mother and then the autonomy or masculine consciousness of father, but neither coming together. What is happening is that the two must come together so that masculine and feminine are in balance. It is no accident that this process of each human coming to terms with his or her own androgyny, his or her own male/femaleness, must occur. There is a sensing of those who are aware and awake that the feminine and the masculine must be balanced. They realize the war must be ended between the male and female polarities so that the autonomy of the masculine principle and the receptivity of the feminine can return to balance.

As the feminine arises again out of the ashes, so to speak, the ancient mysteries of Egypt are returning. And the returning of this knowledge is simply an assistance. What humans choose to do with it is their own free will choice. But the concept is returning and many of you are remembering your roots in ancient Egypt and these earlier times because it is time for the feminine to reawaken. But, let us suggest, the feminine is returning in a different way than before–as a balanced principle–not totally feminine, not totally masculine, but an androgynous merging of the two in balance.

Virginia: If I understood what you said about the feminine principle, does this also have to be applied throughout the solar system or is this primarily a focus only on Earth?

Hathors: This is applied throughout the solar system but at varying times. It is crucial to what is happening on Earth at this moment. You see, there are two parallel processes. Earth as a consciousness is going through her own elevation, a change of herself, so all organisms–not just human, but plant and animal as well–are being affected. These are all going through their own individual processes to align with Earth's shift into a higher vibratory field. The rest of the solar system is also going through a process of changing vibratory fields because your Sun is shifting; however, Earth specifically is going through a unique process that is not being experienced by the other planets at this exact time. That is why there are beings from many dimensions and other realms who are stationed around Earth on planets, asteroids, and inter-dimensional spaces to observe what is happening. It is so unique.

Virginia: I would like to know how Earth and Venus are connected here in the solar system. Was there once a singular consciousness above and beyond those of the physical planetary spheres that we call Venus and Earth? Could you comment on our prior and current relationships with them?

Hathors: Think of Venus as Earth's elder sister. In the formless period before the planets were actually created, the seed or the subtle vibrations of these planets already existed, and there were thought forms and beings moving through these spaces. At that time, the planets of Earth and Venus were intimately connected. They formed a pulsating movement of energy very much like an infinity sign. So Venus and Earth, from their conception, were connected. They are as sister planets. Those of us near Venus who are doing our own work and our own evolution into greater understanding are deeply connected to Earth. Thus, we are committed to assist you, and it is our joy to help those beings who have decided to incarnate on this beautiful planet Earth–as well as to aid the planet herself as she begins to ascend in her own process.

Virginia: I see. We who have studied various metaphysical teachings about the planet Venus have heard the name Sanat Kumara and would like to acknowledge that being and the energies of his teaching from an earlier time period. Is this to be a part of any of your material?

Hathors: We did not plan to discuss our brother Sanat Kumara, but we know him well for it was he who asked us to enter this Universe. Sanat Kumara is an ancient soul who is part of an intergalactic council known as the White Brotherhood. The term white does not refer to skin color, but rather to a state of purity. As an Ascended Master, Sanat Kumara has taken on numerous responsibilities associated with the elevation of planet Earth and this solar system. He has been involved in this task for millennia. He is untiring in his dedication to this realm and he is known throughout the Universe for his powerful magnetic presence. We are quite fond of him especially since he has a most wonderful sense of humor. He is working for the ascension, the evolution of consciousness in the solar system, as are we. His home, if you wish to cite a physical location, would be Venus. But his presence extends through many dimensions, as you are aware. The methods that he uses are in harmony with everything that we plan to reveal in this book. We do not plan to discuss his work or his approach, however, since that would be something deserving of his own message—his own sharing, if you will.

Virginia: In other words there is a companionship of purpose among the higher Venusian energies already established?

Hathors: Yes.

Virginia: We would then like to know if your Venusian experience is related in any way to Sirius planet B or other galactic areas beyond our solar system? And also to Egypt as suggested by the word *Osiris*, *Isis*, and many other Egyptian concepts and words.

Hathors: We will offer our responses to specific questions in that regard, although the material that we have planned for this book does not address that. We are attempting to bring forward practical tools and an understanding that will serve as keys of remembrances and signatures to those who will read the words and recall many things. We desire our information to serve everyone in their own evolution and ascension. But we are open to discussing any questions you have about our history, our background.

To answer your question in regard to Sirius, there is a direct connection between Venus and Sirius, and the connection is that we originally came from Sirius after entering this Universe. The Egyptian Gods to which you refer, such as *Osiris* and *Isis*, would best be described in your terminology as force fields–energy patterns of awareness and vast consciousness. These energies were anthropomorphized by humans in the Egyptian period as *Osiris*, *Isis* and so on. So the Egyptian pantheon is actually a picture, if you will, of force fields that move through the Universe. We would therefore encourage you in these modern times, when you contemplate the Egyptian pantheon, not to take it literally, for the literal understanding was given to the lesser minds of the period. Understand instead, that all teachings are on multiple levels so that what was taken literally by the less evolved consciousness of earlier times was understood by the high priesthood to be symbolic of energies–force fields that moved.

Of course their understanding of these energies was different from your present times, but, essentially, the energy of *Isis* and *Osiris* still remains active and is open to all. This is true of all the pantheon. They are aspects of the One Source. The One Creative Force is all there is– and these are simply aspects or streams of consciousness that move out of the One Source. So, again, it is best to understand that these pantheon deities are benevolent forces that can be aligned with, but they are not the Godhead. They are not the ultimate Source which is without all duality or polarity.

Virginia: Regarding the Hathor influence in ancient

Egypt, you didn't give an approximate date counting backwards from the birth of Christ Jesus. Would this be 20,000, 50,000, 100,000 years or more?

Hathors: It would be longer than that, but in terms of the traces that are left in Egyptian history we go to the period before the Pharaohs. Before Heliopolis, to the time when the sky goddess was *Hator* and the sky god was *Horus*. The location in sequential time would be approximately 10,000 BC (nearly 12,000 years ago).

Virginia: The Egyptian period?

Hathors: The Egyptian period. However, we have worked with this planet prior to that. The Egyptian period is simply one cultural expression of the Mystery. The Mystery is trans-cultural and it extends beyond all times and all places. So we work through those cultures and those belief systems that we encounter...

Virginia: ...who are able and willing to communicate with you?

Hathors: Yes. As ascended beings we are able to traverse wide areas and interact with numerous civilizations. At times we may make contact with only a few individuals. At other times, as in ancient Egypt, we contact and work with thousands. Although some of the information we bring has been preserved in the Egyptian esoteric or hidden teachings, most of our knowledge has yet to be communicated to mankind.

Virginia: Thank you. In terms of Egyptian history then, did the Hathors have anything to do with building the Great Pyramid of Egypt?

Hathors: No, we did not. Regarding the pyramids, they were not merely burial chambers as some of your historians and archaeologists believe. Although many of them actually had burial chambers within them, their primary function was as oscillators of energy. And because the sides of the pyramids originally were burnished, highly polished granite–like marble–this would cause the pyramid to oscillate energy and receive energies. Initiates would enter the pyramids in designated areas that were laid out in specific mathematical ratios. This permitted them to receive understandings of the Great Universe and the Great Mystery that they could not have achieved if they were not in such a matrix of energy. So that was one level.

Another function of the pyramids was energetic. The pyramids were installed in specific mathematical ratios, externally, to facilitate the creation of a grid work. This energetic grid work on the planet was laid for the express purpose of holding the next grid–what is now called the Christ grid–which came into existence when your teacher, known as Jesus of Nazareth, dedicated his efforts. So when this great being entered into his work, the grid that was established by the pyramids supported that new vibration, and that vibrational Christ grid continues to strengthen to this day. So the pyramids were multi-level and multi-purpose devices.

Virginia: I know from being in Guatemala that there are literally hundreds of pyramids scattered through Central America and Mexico, but people don't even know they are there.

Hathors: Yes, they are covered with jungle.

Virginia: So are you saying that these pyramids are positioned around the planet at various points?

Hathors: Yes, but it was not done by one specific civilization. It was done by many different civilizations. But all beings and civilizations that participated in their construction were deeply connected through their intuition and their understanding of the Great Mystery. And they understood energetically what they were doing. But there was no joining together under one chief architect, nor was there a meeting of the chief architects in time and three-dimensional space. This was all done in these various locations but obviously drawing from the same source. They also had outside help.

Virginia: From space?

Hathors: Yes, from the Pleiadians, Sirians, etc.

Virginia: So are you saying that at some point the extraterrestrials worked together? Or that they came at different times?

Hathors: They came at different times. Some of the times overlapped. There is an interesting oddity in your history that can be traced back to the Sirians. In modern Africa there is a tribe known as the Dogon. This tribe has knowledge about Sirius and its smaller "sister." This smaller star was not discovered until the 1960's by your astronomers, but the Dogon have known of it for thousands of years. This knowledge comes from their interactions with the Sirians who came to Africa thousands of years ago as part of their investigation of this planet. The Sirians were, by that time, a highly advanced intergalactic civilization.

Virginia: Thank you. I'd like to be clear that your choices to assist us were not because of previous misdeeds that had to be corrected.

Hathors: Misdeeds on whose parts?

Virginia: Yours and others. Sometimes visitors come from another place and they do things that later perhaps were not in the best interest of the developing consciousness.

Hathors: Oh that (...laughter...). Yes, there were misdeeds done on this planet and that is one reason we were called through the portal of Sirius to this solar system to be your guardians, and elder brothers and sisters. Guardians may not be the right term because some may think that because we are here you do not have to take responsibility. And that is not what we mean! We mean that we hold a certain vibration that is helpful for you as a human civilization—and that vibration is held constant for your support.

Virginia: You mentioned that you originally came *through* Sirius. Could you say more about that?

Hathors: Sirius is a portal from other dimensions of

the Universe which may be difficult to comprehend in terms of three-dimensional space because the portal leads to a non-physical, dimensional space that is our true home. Non-physical dimensional space is a difficult concept for beings living in three dimensions. It would be like the period at the end of this sentence (a two-dimensional space) trying to comprehend the paper on which it appears and the space surrounding the being (you) that is looking at it. It simply does not have a reference point from its own experience to understand anything higher or more complex than two dimensions. Nevertheless, we entered this three-dimensional reality through Sirius.

Sirius is a kind of nexus point for your Universe where the "strands" of your space/time continuum meet and intersect with non-physical hyperspace. This is indeed a strange concept and we could spend a long time discussing it. Since that is not the purpose of this book, let's just say that non-physical hyperspace is a kind of matrix within universal consciousness itself. As consciousness "creates" a universe, it does so by polarizing itself into a nexus point which becomes a physical location in space, which in turn begins the process you call "time." Our true home, if you will, is non-physical hyperspace. However, as we entered this three-dimensional Universe, our first physical home was in the Sirius system. From there we traveled to Venus to be closer to Earth.

Virginia: When you came around 12,000 years ago, that would have been after the fall of Atlantis?

Hathors: Yes, 10,000 B.C. was after the fall of Atlantis. At this time we were actively working in Egypt through the archetypal image of *Hator*. We had also, however, worked with a few highly developed individuals (seers) in both Atlantis and Lemuria. When it became clear that Atlantis and Lemuria would fall, we guided some of these individuals into Egypt. This was done to protect "the Great Work" of alchemy, so that the knowledge and the line of initiates could be protected from devastation. We were not the only intergalactic culture to seed Egypt, by the way. The Arcturians and the Pleiadians also guided some of their human initiates into northern Africa at this time.

Virginia: And when you say you worked with people, what does that mean?

Hathors: We are masters of sound, energy, and love. In relation to humans we work primarily through the feeling nature, what you might call the emotional body. As masters of interdimensional space we can contact humans quite easily. Contact will usually be experienced by you as clairaudient voice transmissions, clairvoyant seeing (visions), intuitions, and appearances in dreams. We made contact with the early Egyptians through the goddess *Hator* which they experienced through mystical visions. Through the cult of the goddess we were able to help the Egyptians create a spiritual Golden Age which culminated in the creation of the Mystery Schools. Through these esoteric centers we were able to assist with the training of initiates, a positive influence which spread throughout the world.

The influence of these Mystery Schools is still active in the world, we might add. Some of these schools are hidden although some of them are becoming public again. The ways in which we "work" vary, but most often one or more of us makes psychic contact with an individual human and begins to instruct him or her according to our understanding. We never impose ourselves. When asked to assist, we will do so, but only within set guidelines. These guidelines insure that we will not interfere with human choice or destiny.

Virginia: Have you had relationships with the Pleiadians or beings from Orion or other so-called outposts of the human family?

Hathors: Yes. We know the Pleiadians, the Sirians, the Orions, and Arcturians. We know others who you do not have names for yet–and we say "yet" because this will change since you are becoming a galactic and inter-galactic humanity. Understand that each of these groups has a distinct flavor–a personality–be they the Pleiadians, the Sirians, etc. So every cultural group has its own specific bent–flavor of personality–as they view and operate through the Great Mystery. And, may we say, these differences give us sincere pleasure! We are intrigued by the differences, by all the levels of the Great Universe, and that is one reason why we are so intrigued and in love with humans.

Virginia: And that's because...?

Hathors: ...of their extreme diversity, their differences, their connection that runs deep to the roots of the Great Universe through their heart, through their emotional being. Yet during incarnation they find themselves in a paradoxical situation–in many ways much more difficult than those of us who are at an ascended level. Why? Because they live in a three-dimensional reality and their senses tell them that things are limited, finite and constricted. Indeed, their senses cannot show them the truth of the Great Universe as we perceive it because their senses are land-locked in this three-dimensional reality. And yet their spirit knows and yearns and is connected to the greater reality, the Greater Mystery. And that to us is something most intriguing–as it is for many other beings in other realms. It is something we cherish and honor in humans.

Virginia: Thank you for that. Could you comment a little bit about your relationship to the solar system in general? You know, we have three smaller planets near Earth–those we call the inner planets which are Mercury, Mars and Venus–and then we have those so-called further-out physical planets of the solar system. Could you give us any background or comment about the settlements on Mercury or Mars? And of course, you've mentioned your own settlements on Venus which I presume were physical at one point.

Hathors: Yes. As to Mars, you will see remnants of the physical structures that they built above ground. There is something you refer to as the "face on Mars" that is actually a structure that existed. There were structures on Venus also, but the settlements on Venus were much older than the ones on Mars, so they are gone. If you go to Venus three-dimensionally you will see nothing but gasses and sand–a very inhospitable place. Mars still has the remnants of the physical structures and there were cultures that lived there. Mars was actually an outpost for many different cultures.

Virginia: Was there one primary outpost in recent times?

Hathors: Let us say this. The history presented to humans by their own sciences is extremely narrow and limited in their perspective and does not have all the pieces of the puzzle. For advanced cultures did exist prior to the early stages of man on this planet. In fact, when man was still very primitive, there were highly advanced inter-galactic, space-traveling civilizations who would come to this solar system on a regular basis to observe the emerging phenomena of life on planet Earth. They would make their outposts at various positions–Mars and Venus being the primary ones.

There were also energetic outposts. This is a different way of looking at things. There are beings who are pure energy and so refined that you would call them ephemeral because they have no form, no mass. Therefore, in the presence of large bodies like Jupiter, they would be relatively unaffected by the gravitational field. So there were beings that also had outposts on Jupiter and Saturn but these were energetic and ephemeral beings and not physical beings like those who came to Mars and Venus.

Virginia: So was Mercury ever an outpost of any kind?

Hathors: Yes. But that was an energetic, ephemeral culture. They were beings specifically able to live off of stellar gas and light. They were very attracted to birthing stars because they fed off them, to use a human term. They drew light and energy, as do all beings, but they were specifically attracted like moths to a flame. They were drawn wherever new stars were birthed and so they existed as an ephemeral, energetic civilization. But there were–and are–some physical three-dimensional structures on Mars. Most traces of them are gone from Venus, but there are still some structures on your Moon which was once a part of Earth long ago.

Virginia: Since the Hathors were especially active in the Egyptian time, what do you think the greatest result of that influence was for humanity?

Hathors: We believe our greatest influence to be that of holding, for humanity, the harmonic of divine love and unconditional acceptance. We also feel that our unique understanding of consciousness has been highly beneficial to mankind. The esoteric teachings we seeded through Egyptian Alchemy have spread throughout the world and into numerous other cultures, finding root in India, China and Tibet. The essence of our teachings, as well as the teachings of other intergalactic and interdimensional civilizations, became incorporated by these cultures as they absorbed the secret teachings of Egypt. You will thus see many parallels between diverse systems of alchemy as expressed through these cultures. Though the language and metaphors of these various systems differ, there are striking similarities.

Probably the most potent of our teachings handed down through these various traditions concerns the lifeforce and how to strengthen and elevate it. This understanding, along with our holding the harmonic of love, may be our two greatest contributions to mankind.

Virginia: Such things are fascinating. Thank you. So in terms of your coming to aid humans on planet Earth, I understand you are here to give practical advice, not just information. Incidentally, in case we do see any of you, could you please describe what a Hathor looks like today, and if our few ancient relics and representations of you found in Egypt are accurate?

Hathors: Well, in my opinion, we are very beautiful, striking beings, but we do have individual differences. We are generally 10-14 of your feet tall, some are taller and some are shorter, and we have rather large heads. We have large ears and we have hair that is pulled back in a stylized fashion which you see in the sculpture shown on this book's cover. We have long hands and long limbs because we are quite tall by Earth standards. As I indicated earlier, our true form is light (as yours is), but as our awareness moves into a denser level of beingness, our light body will take physical body form. In our physical form we take the shape described above.

The ancient artisans of Egypt had various levels of understanding about our appearance, depending on whether or not they were actually in direct communication with us and could sense us clairvoyantly. During the early times of the Egyptian period, before the pharaohs especially, we actually moved on the Earth and those who were working with Hathor energy could see us. We were physically present clairvoyantly, meaning that we would move around the Earth interacting consciously with others, but we could only be seen by the humans with clairvoyant sight. We would not have actual physical form as you know it, but it was so close that we could almost say that we did have physical form here on Earth.

Certain superior artisans who were clearly aware of us did sculpt us and some of these fairly accurate representations appeared on the temple walls and on the columns, especially at the tops of columns. Over time, as the density of this planet increased, the human beings were less able to see us clairvoyantly so they had to rely on things handed down from earlier times. Then the later artisans, who where not directly in communication with us as in earlier times, would stylize their own renditions.

Virginia: In terms of genetics, then, are Hathors humanoid?

Hathors: We are humanoid but our DNA has 12 strands.

Virginia: Since your ears are apparently very sensitive to sound, can you explain how sound became so important to you?

Hathors: What you call "sound" is, to us, the primary vibration in this realm, and we would clarify sound as a vibration not limited to physical sound heard by human ears. When we say "sound," we mean "vibration"–which can occur in a vacuum. Sound as you define it in your physics can only occur where there is a medium to carry a vibration. So sound in our understanding is the ultimate nature and foundation of all reality which is vibratory in nature. In other words, matter is simply vibration at a certain harmonic. Consequently, as one shifts the harmonics one can move out of matter into energy–and one can go back and forth freely when one understands how to do this. The ships that we originally used for space exploration and for entering your solar system were based on sound or vibration. It is a very ancient understanding in our culture and goes back to our roots. We have known this and operated this way for millennia.

Virginia: So now that we have had an introduction to your group is there anything else that any one of your group would like to say before we complete Chapter 1?

Hathors: We would like to express our deepest gratitude to our brothers and sisters in human form who have come to this planet at this time to pass through the great portal of change and shift to a new dimension of consciousness. Knowing, as we do, how difficult this is, how challenging–but also how rewarding–we stand on the other side of time, as it were, with our arms outstretched to welcome you into the intergalactic realms–into the subtler realms of life. We bring this material to you in greatest humility with the hope that it may be of service to you. If something can be used by you, so be it. If the things we share do not touch you, then pass them by. Whatever your choice, we honor you at this moment, which is charged with opportunities for an evolutionary unfolding that has not been seen in this Universe since the beginning of time.

Virginia: Thank you very much. We are grateful for your concern and support.

Chapter 2
The Human as an Energy System

As your elder brothers and sisters, we live in what you would term the fourth dimension–another frequency domain. And so our view or perspective of you is unique because we perceive you through an energy state that is different than yours. We are aware of you in terms of your interpenetrating fields of energy.

The first of these fields, which is obvious to you, is what you would term your physical body with all its various chemical, biochemical, and electrical processes extending through the trillions and trillions of cells that make up the space of your body. However, when we see your physical body we see it mostly in terms of space. We see it as a galaxy of stars, for each atom unto itself is much like a solar system with the central sun as the nucleus and the planets as electrons spinning around. The hermetic alchemists which came out of the Egyptian tradition spoke of the law, "As above, so below," meaning that in all levels of creation, each level is replicated below it and above it. Thus the solar system is a movement of planets around the central Sun and in the atom, the electrons move around the central nucleus. As your solar system is mostly space, so are you.

Indeed, there is a tremendous amount of space within your physical body and it is an illusion that you are solid. Even your science has uncovered that you are more than *99 percent* space. When we sense your physical body we see it as spatial, not solid. Consequently we do not sense your physical body in the same way as you do.

We literally see you as a walking, moving galaxy of stars. So although this first field seems very physically solid to you, it is actually quite different from the standpoint of light, of energy.

Interpenetrating this physical field is a second field of energy that we call the *"Ka"* which would be, in your understanding, the *pranic* body. *Prana*, as uncovered by the yogis of ancient traditions, is the essential life-force in oxygen but is not merely what you term oxygen. *Prana* is amplified in large areas of vegetation and in large bodies of moving water. *Prana* is the life-force, and this *prana* interpenetrates both the physical body and the *pranic* body which we call the *Ka*. This *Ka* is actually the source of the life-force moving through the first level of the physical field, the physical body. The *Ka* is sometimes called the spiritual or etheric twin since it is a duplicate of the physical body and its energetic fields, but at a subtler state of energy. Those familiar with Egyptian Alchemy will recognize the term *"Ka"* which is the energy twin that can temporarily survive the physical body after death, though it is not the immortal soul.

Without the *prana* moving through your physical body and amplifying the *Ka*, you would not be able to live. It is the very force of life itself. Therefore, some of the techniques we will be sharing with you are actually techniques to stabilize the *pranic* flow within the galaxy that you call your physical body—which is essential for health, for existence!

Although you have other subtle bodies called the emotional, causal and astral bodies, we will focus primarily on the *Ka*, since development of this body will give you a tremendous movement to higher consciousness.

Looking at Diagram #1a & 1b, please note that all bipolar magnetic fields have similar shapes. Bipolar magnetic fields include such diverse forms as bar magnets, apples, planets (including Earth) and human beings.

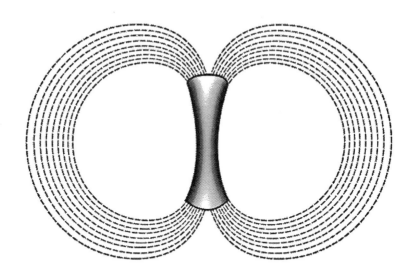

Diagram 1a – A two-dimensional representation of a bi-polar magnetic field (i.e., bar magnet).

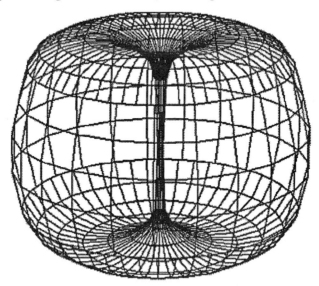

Diagram 1b – A three-dimensional representation of a bi-polar magnetic field, sometimes referred to as a "tube torus." Imagine one around your own body.

In Diagram #1c you will see a two-dimensional representation of the electromagnetic field surrounding the human body. Your human body, then, is a bipolar magnet with its central column sometimes referred to as the *central channel*, the *middle column*, the *pranic tube*, or the *antakarana* by various ancient esoteric traditions. All bipolar magnets, as your science has uncovered, emit a field that three-dimensionally resembles a donut-like shape called a "tube torus." This field actually moves around the body three-dimensionally.

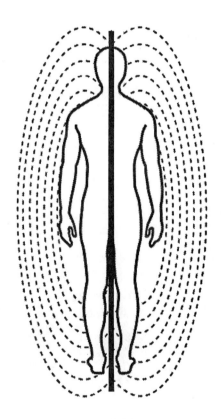

Diagram 1c - A two-dimensional representation of the human bi-polar magnetic field.

Going right down through the middle of the tube, the middle of this donut-like shape, is a channel of energy. This is actually the central column of the magnetic field that is emitted by the physical body. So this central column is the middle conduit, if you will, of an electromagnetic field that is the basis of life. In their esoteric understanding, many different cultures have touched upon and developed techniques involving this central column or *pranic* tube, as it is sometimes called.

Therefore, in terms of yourself as an energy system, the key central field to turn your attention to, from our understanding, is the *Ka*–the *pranic* body. How you draw in or do not draw in life-force (*prana*) determines how much energy is available to your organs and bodily systems. The *Ka* determines the clarity, the power, and the impact of your thought; and it also determines the quality of your emotion. If the *Ka* is disturbed then the other fields are disturbed–the physical body operates at a lesser level of energy, thought is diminished and emotions become perturbed. Then how do you bring more *prana* into the *Ka* so that it radiates out into the physical galaxy of your body and into the other subtle bodies, as well? This is the central question that we would now wish to answer.

The key lies in the *pranic* tube that extends down through the center of your body. This *pranic* tube roughly corresponds to a pathway that the yogis, in your tradition of this planet, called the "*sushumna.*" The *sushumna* is the pathway by which the *kundalini* energy or life-force rises from the base of the spine, up through the various energy centers of the body (the *chakras*), into the head center.

Here it meets the crown and opens consciousness to what would be termed "cosmic consciousness" or the connection to All That Is–a very highly elevated state of consciousness! Although the energy of the life-force moves up through this pathway called the *sushumna*, if you do a physical dissection of the body, you will not find it. It is a subtle energy. But it exists. It is as real as anything else in your world except that it is at a frequency domain that is outside the *one percent* of reality that you can perceive through your senses. However, the *pranic* tube, unlike the *sushumna*, does not follow the path of the spine, but forms a straight line from the crown (at the top of the head) down through the perineum (a point midway between the genitals and the anus). (See Diagram 2)

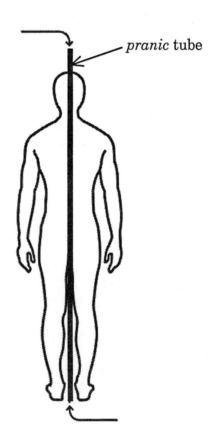

pranic tube

Diagram 2 - The movement of energy and/or light into the *pranic* tube down from heaven or up from Earth.

This *pranic* tube actually extends into the Earth. Depending upon the development of your consciousness, it will either be connected just slightly above the Earth's surface, connected down below it just a few inches, or it can connect down to the very core of the Earth itself. This *pranic* tube also extends above the head and can go up several feet or several thousand miles, again depending upon the state of consciousness of the being. Generally speaking, if you touch your thumb and second finger together and make a circle, your *pranic* tube will be about the size of that circle. It does not bend with the spine. It extends, we can safely say in the way that we will be working with you, from the top of the head down through the perineum. This *pranic* tube focus is the primary method we would utilize with you in developing your capacity to activate the *Ka*, to increase the flow of *prana* throughout the physical body.

Now, for your benefit, we would share three specific techniques to build the *Ka*, and then some thoughts concerning things we recommend you *increase* in your life and things we recommend you *decrease* in your life. Understand that you have free choice in this, and we make no judgment about what you choose to do or not do. From our perspective, if you wish to build the *Ka*, there are things you must do and things you must avoid. It is that simple. So let us turn our attention to the techniques to begin the process of becoming aware of the *Ka* and the *pranic* tube so that you can begin to build the energy mastery necessary for health and higher consciousness.

๛๛๛๛ SELF-MASTERY EXERCISE #1 ๛๛๛๛
๛ PART A ๛

In the first exercise (see Diagram 2) you inhale up through the pranic tube that is connected to the Earth. You breathe up into the pranic tube from the Earth with one breath and then you relax and let it go with a sigh. Then with the second breath, you

*breathe in from above the head, bringing celestial
energy down into the body's pranic tube and then
again you release the breath and sigh. Try this several times until you clearly sense a flow of energy
into the pranic tube.*

All you're doing in this first step is to begin to sense
the subtle flow of energy–the *prana*–moving up from the
Earth and into the *pranic* tube, and then down from the
celestial realm into the *pranic* tube. It is probably easier
if you play some type of relaxing music since many people
find that music supports their ability to relax, to turn in-
ward, and thus allows them to facilitate this process.
However, it can certainly be done without music, particularly by those who enjoy quiet time. It is especially
powerful when done outdoors in the purity of nature.

The *Ka* is crucial to the process of raising your vibration in the ascending spiral of consciousness, which we
will discuss more thoroughly later on. The process of moving your entire being up the ascending spiral requires
energy. It requires force, life-force. And that life-force is
generated through the *Ka*. The actual source of the life-
force comes from All That Is and it emanates through all
the particles and energetic streams that move through
the Universe. We are sure that you can identify times in
your life when you have felt low in your life-force. Your
physical body would not function very well. Your emotional
body felt disturbed. Perhaps you had erratic thoughts, difficulty focusing your attention, or impingements from the
astral world in the form of strange dreams–dreams that
may have even intruded into conscious awareness during
your waking hours.

In such cases, what has happened is that the *Ka* was
so depleted that it could not radiate out into the physical
body, into the mental body, and the emotional body, thereby
creating the appropriate boundaries for these bodies. Since
the converse is also true, it is advisable to form a relationship with the *Ka*, with the *pranic* body, so that everything

is calculated to reinforce your life-force. What you eat, what you drink, who you interact with, and the thoughts and emotions you entertain build or diminish the *Ka*. If you deliberately cause the *pranic* body to intensify and radiate into the physical body, then you will be prepared to begin the ascension process as we define it.

❧ PART B ❧

The next step in this Self-Mastery Exercise is to draw the prana into the pranic tube and then to <u>circulate it through the physical body</u>. (See Diagram 3)

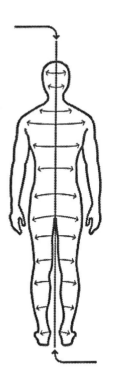

Step 1: *As you did before, draw the prana up from the Earth into your pranic tube as you inhale. Hold the breath for just a moment and then exhale with a sigh. Focus your attention on the pranic tube.*

Step 2: *Now inhale, drawing prana down from above the head into the pranic tube. Hold the breath for a moment while you focus on the pranic tube. Exhale and sigh as you shift your awareness to your entire physical body. The prana will then flow out from the pranic tube into your body by the Law of Attention (i.e., "Energy follows awareness"). Work with this until you sense a flow of energy from the pranic tube out into the physical body.*

Diagram 3 - The movement of "celestial energy" and "Earthly energy" into the *pranic* tube and from there into the physical body.

When you first begin the process it may be a very subtle sensation and some areas of your body will be more sensitized to the flow of *prana* than others. But eventually you will have the distinct physical sensation of the *prana* moving out into the physical body. As your awareness becomes more subtle, you may notice the *prana* moving into the subtle bodies as well. Let it interpenetrate and extend outward from your actual physical body. This allows you to truly increase the *Ka*, to intensify the *pranic* body.

After you have been able to master this level, you are ready to go to the third part. And the third part is the *qualification* of the energy you are bringing in through a specific emotional vibratory field. This field creates a high level of coherence in your system and is the strongest, most reinforcing vibratory field you can establish. This ideal quality–this emotional, vibrational field–is what you call *"unconditional acceptance"* or *"unconditional love."* So this is the third step after you feel you have mastered Parts A and B above. *Do not rush into Part C until you fully and clearly feel the sensation of prana moving through the pranic tube and out into the physical body.*

Once you have attained the sensation of moving *prana*, the next step is to bring your awareness to the heart center which is in the center of the chest, located right in front of the *pranic* tube. With your awareness in the heart center, recall the emotion of unconditional acceptance or unconditional love. The heart center or the heart *chakra* is not the same as the physical heart. The heart *chakra* is an energy vortex in the center of the chest which has recently been scientifically measured and quantified. Indeed, scientific studies indicate that the *chakra*s emit both sound and color. (For further information, see Brain States by Tom Kenyon, U.S. Publishing.)

❧ PART C ❧

Step 1: *Now place your awareness in the heart chakra at the center of the chest. Recall a feeling of* *unconditional love and acceptance. Make sure you're actually* *feeling* *this state.* *Thinking about it* *will not do.*

Step 2: *With your awareness in the heart center and holding the feeling-state of unconditional love and acceptance, inhale and draw prana* *up from the Earth* *into your pranic tube. Hold the breath for a moment as you focus on the pranic tube, still holding the feeling-state of love and acceptance. When you exhale, move your awareness into the physical body and allow the "qualified prana" to move out from the pranic tube into the entire body. (See Diagram 4)*

Step 3: *Return your awareness to the heart center and, holding the feeling-state of unconditional love and acceptance once again, inhale and draw prana* *down from the space above your head* *into the pranic tube. Hold the breath for a moment, and focus on the pranic tube, still holding the feeling-state of love and acceptance. When you exhale, move your awareness into the physical body and allow the "qualified prana" to move out from the pranic tube into the body.*

Diagram 4 - The heavenly and Earthly energies move into the *pranic* tube and then to the heart center or *chakra*. The "qualified" energies are then circulated throughout the body.

Now, we realize that some readers may not have experienced true unconditional love or unconditional acceptance. For those of you who are in this position, set aside Part C of the exercise for now. Continue to work with the first two parts of the exercise (drawing *prana* into the *pranic* tube and circulating it through the body), and don't worry about qualifying the energy for now. By the time you finish our discussion and exercises, you will find it much easier to access the feeling-states of unconditional love and acceptance.

For those of you who were able to access the feeling-states of unconditional love and acceptance, add this part to your practice. You will find that it both strengthens your life-force and your sense of well-being.

However, you must actually practice this exercise for it to work. If you hold it as just another idea or concept, you will not affect the *Ka*. *You must practice it.*

We indicated that there were things that we would like to discuss, from our understanding, that both improve and strengthen the *Ka* and also things that diminish it. And if you wish to take this ascension journey, you will need to make the *Ka* as strong as possible. There are very clear guidelines, and of course if you choose not to practice them, that is fine. There is no judgment. It is all free will and free choice. But if you wish to begin the ascension spiral through the different levels of your own being, you must strengthen your *Ka* and also realize that there are ways you can harm yourself.

For example, if you have a bucket and you fill it with water from a well and your goal is to take it to the garden and put it into the roots of the plants, you don't punch holes in the bottom of the bucket and then try to carry water back to the garden, do you? No, because by the time you get there the water will be gone. It is wasted effort. It is the same thing with this. These are only the first steps; there are many more advanced steps, but these first steps will put you well on the road to building your life-force.

We are not telling you to do or not to do anything! We want to be very clear that you have free will and that your choices are your own responsibility. We're simply saying that from our experience in this process–and we have gone through this process–there are things that will help or hinder your ability to ascend through the different levels of your being. There are even things that will damage the *Ka*, and we want to let you know what those are so you can make an insightful decision about your actions and behaviors.

The first thing we shall discuss has to do with the life-force you express sexually. The sexual energy is actually the manifestation of *Ka* through the lower centers–in terms of orientation, not in terms of value–meaning it is appropriately expressed through the genitals as procreation or as sexual pleasure. However, in building the *Ka*, you want to raise that energy by methods that will allow you to experience sexual bliss and ecstasy *without depleting the life-force*.

The ancient techniques for raising this energy can be found in books on Taoist yoga, tantric yoga, and *kundalini* yoga, so we won't go into those here. We would say that in using our methods, which became the underpinnings of Egyptian Alchemy, you literally raise the life-force into your higher centers by bringing that life-force into all of your body. If you allow the *pranic* life-force to express itself as a release of sexual fluids and energy only, then the *prana* is released through those lower centers, is not elevated, and will not have a long term positive effect upon the *Ka*.

If you express your sexuality too often through the sexual act without retaining the sexual energy so it can circulate upward, you actually deplete the *Ka*. This will, in turn, deplete the organs of your physical body, deplete the immune system, and create other various decreases of energy within yourself as an energy system. Let us be very clear, however, that we are not saying to deny yourself sexual pleasure. There are methods that have been developed by Taoist sages and tantric yogis which allow you to experience profound states of sexual bliss and ecstasy without depleting the *Ka*. In fact, these practices strengthen your life-force and elevate consciousness. We suggest you explore these methods.

Another thing affecting the *Ka* is the type of food that you eat and the type of fluids you drink–for the life-force comes in from many areas. Generally speaking, humans have a tendency to get very agitated when someone tells them what they should do or not do in terms of dietary habits because people have great attachments to food. So we will give you a broad guideline here leaving you to choose your path.

Generally speaking, to build the *Ka*, eating "live" foods will assist the process, but you want to do this in balance. If you're not used to eating live foods–meaning uncooked vegetables and fruits, as well as sprouted grains, *slowly begin this change*. Add live foods to your diet in a way that feels comfortable. Adding too much live food, without proper preparation, (i.e., not giving your body a chance to adjust to the higher enzyme levels) can lead to a detoxification crisis. As in all things, moderation is best. Listen carefully to your body, not to your personality whims. Your body will tell you what it needs and what is best.

This may seem paradoxical, but when you reach a certain point in consciousness, you can eat anything without negative effects. Ultimately, food has very little to do with spiritual evolution. However, our advice is given for the average person who wishes to strengthen his or her *Ka*. Most people will experience an increase in vitality if they start adding some live foods to the diet. As a general principle, life-force is only increased by other life-forces. Your "fast foods" are dead. And those items you call "convenience foods" generally deplete the *Ka* because they require so many digestive enzymes to process these "dead" food stuffs. You see, *one of the major drains on the pranic fire, on the pranic body, is the digestive process.*

Much *prana* is actually required to digest food, especially meat. What happens is that the *prana* gets stepped-down from the *Ka's* faster vibratory field into the physical body's digestive process with its system of ductless and ducted glands, requiring many digestive enzymes to be produced and secreted. This is a strain on your energy. So watching what you eat, and eating as purely and cleanly as possible will reinforce the *Ka*. Pure water is also critical, as is exercise. In addition, be around nature as much as possible, breathing fresh air that is unpolluted and allowing yourself to be safely exposed to sunlight, especially through your eyes. This means wearing sunglasses as little as possible unless the Sun is so very bright that you really need to protect your eyes. These are just some very simple suggestions to incorporate into your life, should you wish. In no way are we giving medical advice or suggesting unsafe experimentation.

You will find, as you build the *Ka*, the *pranic* force, and as you hold the intention to elevate yourself in consciousness, that you will begin to have intuitions and inner understandings about things that are very valuable. This is called "*gnosis.*" *Gnosis* means "knowledge," and it comes as a feeling, a sudden "knowing." *Gnosis*, then, is a refinement of your feeling nature which naturally evolves as the *Ka* is strengthened, and which provides a deeper soul connection.

Now we pause to ask for your questions, Virginia.

Virginia: Would you like to add some further comments in this chapter about what would help increase our *Ka*? I sense that you have an enormous reservoir of information about this topic.

Hathors: Well, we are glad you asked that because there are so many areas to work in which can strengthen the *Ka*. But we're a little timid, knowing human nature as we do, about giving a list of things to avoid, lest people become rebellious.

Virginia: Understood. But I encourage your full comment for those who can benefit.

Hathors: We have noticed a tendency for many people to overstimulate themselves, to push themselves beyond their physical limit. When you are fatigued and you push yourself further through artificial means such as stimulants, your *Ka* can get depleted. As the physical body reserves get depleted, this eventually sets up a very negative set of circumstances leading to physical problems. Beyond that, if the *Ka* becomes depleted, you cannot move forward along the ascending spiral. So it's a balance of rest, exercise and movement, wise choices about what to eat and drink, and consciously maintaining positive thoughts and actions.

Of course, the types of people you associate with also have an effect on your *Ka*. Those who are positive, vital, and uplifting in their nature tend to reinforce your *Ka*, whereas those who are negative, pessimistic, and depleted will tend to deplete you. So making decisions about those with whom you live and work, based on *Ka*, is another aspect. Please understand that we are not giving you a new list of Ten Commandments to follow! We want to avoid that, but we do encourage you to remember that finding your balance is vital–and that's the intention behind our comments in these important areas.

Virginia: I wonder if you might also discuss safe healing practices for those people who share their healing energies with others? Things like acupressure, massage, various body work techniques, as well as the laying on of hands, faith healing, etc. These kinds of healing using personal touch are becoming very popular in America.

Hathors: Well, let us give a little caution here to all but the very purest of healers. We would say to healers that you need to be aware that there is a very distinct possibility of danger when working with other people's energy *unless you are very pure*. For example, an improperly purified healer who works with someone who is ill may actually feel depleted after working with this person. Or they may later have a healing crisis themselves to face.

Some healers may discover to their dismay that after they have brought through healing energies for another person, their own *Ka* is depleted although they do not feel the result immediately. The reason for this, from our understanding, has to do with where the healing energy is coming from and the state of personal unawareness the healer is in. Essentially what happens is when a person is in need of energy there is a level of self (not necessarily conscious) that pulls energy from whomever and whatever is available. If you are a healer and you are with someone who is in need of a type of energy that you have, they will pull it from you either consciously or unconsciously.

Virginia: Are you speaking of highly subtle energies or more physical body energies?

Hathors: We are speaking about subtle energy–*the vital energy (prana)* which is held by the *Ka*, the spiritual twin of the physical body. Because the *Ka* holds life-force and vitality, a healer, if she or he is proficient, is basically a vital, fully-charged individual.

When your energy fields–your "luminous eggs"–are interconnected, there are strands sent from the one who needs energy to the one who has energy. The needy one pulls energy like water from a well. And this is usually an unconscious thing because it automatically happens at another level of self. Indeed, this is the true symbolic meaning of the word vampire. You can be "vampired" of your energy. And we're not talking about sucking someone's blood; we are talking about pulling someone's vital energy from their *Ka*.

If you are not prepared and don't understand this, you can be with someone who is physically and/or emotionally depleted, or who may be psychologically disturbed, and after you leave them you feel depleted yourself. This is one reason why some nurses, doctors and other healthcare givers often feel drained. They are frequently surrounded by the sick who drain their *Ka* for healing energy. Transfusions of energy, not just blood, are possible. So this is the first level of energy. It's a vitality that can be pulled or drained by another person. If you are not aware of your *Ka* and how it's being extracted from you, then you may suddenly feel as if the plug has been pulled–there is no energy left in your body–so you must go off and replenish it.

Another level of energy depletion is not directly related to the *Ka*, but is related instead to the subtle "emotional flows" within one's emotional body. These "emotional flows" are affected by the healer's thoughts and feelings about the person being healed. These "emotional flows" can also be the result of the healer's "agendas"…in other words, a purposeful strategy by which a healer is trying to "force" a healing through his or her own will. As a healer, one needs to be very clear mentally and emotionally as to where the healing is coming from and why one is in the act of "healing" another. Even the innocent desire to help, to be a good person, or to be a hero are potential contaminants, as well as possible sources of distortion and depletion.

If you as a healer are sending the energy from yourself, from your own vitality, then of course you are in trouble because you personally have only a limited amount of energy that is available to you until you replenish it.

Virginia: Like a battery system.

Hathors: Yes. A very apt metaphor. If you are very clear that you're a channel for the *prana*, the energy…that the healing energy simply flows *through* you and not *from* you–then you're not giving away your own energy but merely channeling the energy from a higher source. If it flows through you without the blockages of limiting motives, this purity will reduce much of the fatigue and exhaustion that some healers are experiencing.

Virginia: Let me be explicit here. Are you confirming our current teachings that say that these more subtle energies should flow only from a higher source through the healer?

Hathors: Yes. *Prana*, or the fundamental energy of life is omnipresent and can be funneled or channeled from the omnipresent Source of energy. One does not have to use one's own energy to give to another. Always be clear that you are drawing from the greater Source. The other issue is being clear about your own *Ka* and your own lifeforce so that you can sense when your energy is being drawn from you. Unfortunately, most humans are not aware when their energy is being "vampired" or pulled from them until after the fact, until they are exhausted.

Virginia: Now, we don't want to discourage people who are compassionate and who desire to be useful to others. What summary can you give to encourage people as they learn to become healers?

Hathors: We suggest a simple method for protecting yourself when "healing" another person. You simply focus some part of your attention on the *pranic* tube that goes through the center of your body (as discussed in the first exercise in this chapter). This tube connects you to both heaven and Earth. And by connecting the two through your own body, the omnipresent healing energy will more fully move through you and you will, at the same time, be more grounded, balanced, and aware.

Virginia: If someone who thinks of him or herself as a healer is going through physical or emotional difficulties in their own life, is it likely to be harmful to attempt to give energy away at that time?

Hathors: It's harmful for them to give energy away at any time.

Virginia: Understood. My question was poorly stated. Is it likely that the healer, in their stress and emotional upset, would have a tendency to be imbalanced and not even notice it?

Hathors: Yes. When one is physically weary, feeling low or emotionally worried, it is best not to work with another person. Be honest and tell the other person your situation.

Virginia: Rather than force yourself to be available inappropriately?

Hathors: Yes. It's a disservice to the one receiving the healing energy; because if you are emotionally disturbed, your emotional body is vibrating and holding patterns and energies of limitation. If the person has come to receive healing, their *Ka* is probably depleted to begin with and they may take on your negativity, your imbalanced energies.

Virginia: So coming back to ways in which healers could test themselves before offering healing—if they've been sick or in some kind of upset or emotional difficulties—they should take a reflective time to check themselves out to see if they're really capable of doing their best work?

Hathors: Yes, and it usually only takes a few moments to check in with oneself and get a very clear, honest assessment.

Virginia: So, following any healing session with another person, it's good to double check to be sure that the healer has really received energy from the highest level and that their own energy level is okay?

Hathors: Yes.

Virginia: To re-cap—we've said that checking one's energy and emotional state before one attempts to give healing energy to another, is a very good thing to do. Then, following a healing session, the healer should check and be sure their energy level is high and they haven't lost something along the way.

Hathors: Yes, and we would also add that, as a healer, you need to cultivate an awareness of your own *Ka*, your own vitality. It is possible, by the way, for a person to pull on another individual's energy even if they are not within the proximity of each other physically–it can be done from thousands of miles away. As a healer is working with a person, it would be a higher level of mastery to monitor one's own vital force while the healing session is going on. That way, the healer can sense if there is any drain on their vital energy and make adjustments immediately, rather than after depletion occurs. Obviously, it is far easier to accommodate and adjust for depletion before one is truly physically exhausted.

Virginia: Agreed. Is there anything else you'd like to say about healing energies, the *Ka,* and the more subtle frequencies before we leave that topic?

Hathors: The highest healing comes from the Source of All That Is–the One beyond the duality, what the Egyptians called *"Neter Neteru,"* the Supreme Being, the Godhead, whatever words you use. For obvious reasons it is better to use the infinite reservoir of the Source rather than one's own energy. The *prana* is not the most subtle energy even though it is more subtle than physical matter. There are energies that are closer to the Supreme Being in vibration; these energies have more powerful healing properties. So the higher one ascends in vibration, to use that term, the closer one will get to the Source where one can then draw on those subtle energies. The purer you are, the more powerful your healing results will be.

Virginia: Because those high energies will contain the composite of all that is needed?

Hathors: Yes.

Virginia: Right now in what we call the healing interest groups, there are quite a variety of patterns in which people simply infuse energy–presumably from a higher source which flows through their own beingness to others–which we've been discussing. At the same time, there also seems to be an awakening in some healers that helps them notice spiritual, psychic energy blockages that a person is holding, either at the physical or emotional level, which is causing the depletion of energy. So is there anything you'd like to say about the way in which healers themselves may be discovering a higher evolutionary understanding about the use of energy?

Hathors: As a healer's mastery evolves, he or she reaches the point where it is possible to dissolve an energetic block or dissolve a crystallized pattern through a skillful manipulation of energy. This level of mastery is a natural development. However, there is a fine line between seeing the need for a change and forcing that change. The healer must ascertain whether the time is "ripe" for the change or not. In the final analysis the choice for this change must come from the one being healed and not from the healer. Healers who impose their will onto others, even to be helpful, will find that such manipulations, no matter how skillfully applied, are ultimately ineffective.

Healers must also understand that there is no accident in who comes to them for healing The persons they attract to themselves are often a reflection of the healer's own psycho-spiritual issues. So in the process of healing and being a conduit for higher energies, the healer is also a learner. If healers remain humble and open to their clients as reflections of their own "process," they can grow even more in self-awareness and compassion. Finally, healers need to be clear that others have a right to suffer. Do not impose your timetables onto another. Grant the space and the grace for others to move into greater awareness at their own speed.

Do you have any further questions?

Virginia: Yes. One question did come to mind when you were discussing the opportunity of using sexual energy for consciousness advancement. Does this apply to the increasing numbers of people who are called homosexual? How can a man safely have sex with a man? And how can two women use sex to expand their consciousness without the sharing of semen? What have you noticed that could be spoken to guide these individuals?

Hathors: There is nothing intrinsically limiting about the homosexual or lesbian lifestyle in terms of the *Ka* if the sexual energy is elevated. If men, in a sexual relationship with each other, were to practice the ancient Taoist and tantric methods for sexual pleasure without ejaculating–they would strengthen the *Ka*, elevate the sexual energy to the higher centers, and experience more intense levels of pleasure. When the sexual energies are elevated, it is possible for every cell of the body to go into orgasmic ecstasy. Men generally confine orgasm to the pelvic area, but as they work with these ancient methods, they will discover that orgasm need not be limited to this one area.

Generally speaking, a woman's vitality, her *Ka*, is stronger than a man's. This is genetically determined since women have to lend their *Ka* if they carry children. The foetus actually draws upon the mother's *Ka* to develop and to be birthed. This is one reason that mothers and their children often have powerful and deep bonds to each other. So women are predisposed to having stronger *Ka*'s than men. They also tend to be more sensitive to cellular orgasm, though men can certainly develop this ability.

Women in sexual relationships with each other can use the sexual energy to expand their consciousness by bringing the rush of orgasm up the *pranic* tube during orgasm and from there, circulating it through the body. The Taoist and tantric methods used by women are similar for those used by men except that, of course, there is no need to retain semen.

From an energetic standpoint, all persons are both male and female. At the subtle levels of energy and consciousness, you are potentially androgynous, meaning "balanced between" the sexual polarities of your being. And thus it is not necessary, from an alchemical standpoint, to have a partner in order to elevate your sexual energy.

Virginia: Thank you. For those readers who are or

would be celibate, is there any comment you could make about celibacy's relationship to ascension?

Hathors: The ancient understanding of celibacy has, for the most part, been lost. In the Mystery Schools of ancient Egypt there were certain periods when the initiate was temporarily required to remain celibate. The purpose was to allow students to explore their own sexually-based energy patterns. By entering these realms of the self, the initiate could facilitate the merging of the male and female aspects, an event termed the "alchemical marriage." Now, however, celibacy has simply become avoidance or suppression without any understanding of the energetics involved.

You don't need a sexual relationship to reach high states of consciousness, since the sexual energy can be circulated internally without the need of a partner. If one practices celibacy and at the same time stimulates the life-force to rise from the root and sexual centers (near the base of the spine), one will experience bliss and ecstasy. As the released energy moves up the spine into the higher centers, it opens higher states of awareness and consciousness. For those choosing the celibate path, we would encourage learning how to circulate one's sexual energy internally. True celibacy is not suppression, but rather a raising up of the life-force.

Within you is a power and a mystery–the power and mystery of life itself. It is a precious gift that has been given. Cherish it. Honor it. Fathom it with your heart and mind. May you find its Source, and may that Source lift you up into the heavenly realms of consciousness!

Chapter 3
Feeling and Human Evolution

We would like to share a concept that will accelerate your evolution. It has to do with what you term "feeling." For us, we draw distinction between feeling and emotion. Feeling includes the physical sensations that you experience–both physical sensations of the sensory world and physical sensations of the inner or subtle worlds. We define emotion as a combination of feelings with thoughts about those feelings. For instance, if the weather is cool and overcast, your feeling nature will report that particular information about the environment. Your feeling nature receives this information through the body's nervous system. In addition, the subtle bodies will receive information which will translate as feeling.

If you happen to have a negative thought about it being a cool, overcast day, then you might judge or decide "this is a dreary day," and you might find yourself having a depressed feeling. This occurs because you have responded judgmentally to a neutral feeling received, in innocence, through your feeling nature. Interestingly, someone else might really enjoy a cool, overcast day and be uplifted by the very thought of it.

True feelings are neither positive nor negative. They are simply neutral reports, a kind of barometer about what is happening in your own energy-responsive, energy-attuned world.

Your feeling nature is an attribute of your emotional body which is closely tied to the *Ka*. The emotional body is a field of energy that surrounds and interpenetrates your physical body. When something activates the emotional body it begins to vibrate in specific ratios setting off "energy flows" which stream around and through the physical body. If these flows are strong enough (i.e., when a strong feeling/emotional reaction occurs), these flows can be physically felt within the tissues of the body itself–thus the stronger the feeling response the stronger the physical sensation. One of the keys to the ascension process, from an energetic standpoint, is to allow your energy fields to open and to move freely. The ability to move more energy and to master positive movement of that energy comes through cultivation of your feeling nature.

Your emotions have an effect on health which is being more clearly demonstrated and documented in your sciences. And there is one vital, specific, and positive resonance that takes place when a person feels a certain kind of emotion–an emotional vibratory field called unconditional acceptance or unconditional love. This sets up an intercellular resonance that positively affects the DNA, making it stronger, helping it code information more precisely. This positive resonance actually emerges whenever you feel the emotion of unconditional acceptance or love. Naturally, the more you experience this emotion, the more you benefit all levels of your total self...from the DNA...from the physical level of your body...through the emotional body...to reinforcement of the *pranic* body of the *Ka*...and also to feelings of well-being. Allowing the energy of unconditional acceptance and love to move through the emotional body activates a process of profound healing and balance.

Allowing yourself to experience all feelings and emotions is a powerful means to move energy through your *Ka*. What happens for many human beings, however, is that in a difficult or challenging situation they mentally label that situation as "bad," and resist the resulting emotions. When you resist feelings or emotions, your emotional body cannot vibrate properly and it "freezes" or locks-up. When it is not able to move or vibrate properly, you become less aware mentally and your thoughts get fuzzy, unclear and muddled.

The life situations that arise today on your planet and the emotions they generate are actually the initiatory phases of higher consciousness leading to ascension and mastery. In the ancient temples of Egypt, an initiate on the path to higher consciousness would go through different initiations, each becoming more and more intense. Today, however, your daily life is this process of initiation.

There is no place that you need to go to receive initiations, for you are being initiated by life wherever you are. The key is allowing yourself to be aware of your feelings and emotional responses to situations so they can be noticed and balanced. Because the emotional body and the *Ka* are energetically connected, by strengthening your *Ka* and by bringing your emotions and feelings into full and positive awareness, you greatly accelerate your own evolution.

The emotional body has its own resonance and moves differently than the *Ka*. Because it vibrates at a different frequency rate, it responds to, and holds, information differently. This is so important that we wish to take you through an experience. It will provide you, we hope, with an appreciation of how your emotional body holds memory and how emotional patterns are expressed so that you can rise to the place of mastery and shift out of difficult emotional spaces more quickly.

So we would ask, Virginia, before we proceed to the techniques, are there any questions you anticipate our readers might have?

Virginia: Thank you. You haven't said much about the size and shape of our other various subtle body fields, those beyond the physical level. Can you describe the way you view them as you look at us when we're at our

strongest energies? And what it looks like when our energies are not operating properly?

Hathors: With the exception of the physical body,
the various other interpenetrating fields are like luminous egg-shaped fields of light and they are imbedded in
each other. The *Ka* is actually a complex field of energy.
Its primary form is similar to that of the physical body
though slightly larger. This is why it is called the "etheric
or spiritual twin" in Egyptian Alchemy. The early Egyptians understood its nature and relationship to the
physical form. Indeed, the *Ka* can move about and even
bi-locate (in which a person appears to be in two places at
the same time). The *Ka* also has an auric field of energy
around it which we call the *pranic* body.

When we refer to the *Ka* we often mean both its primary form and its auric field. This field is egg-shaped,
much like the other fields, and can get quite large as a
person moves upward in consciousness. *This auric field
around the Ka can ignite at a certain moment in the upward movement of ascension and become a field of intense
golden light.* The early Egyptians referred to this as the
"*sahhu*" or glorious spiritual body. However, we are speaking here of very advanced energy states.

Generally speaking, for most people, the *pranic* body
extends from a few inches to several feet from the physical body. The emotional body is the next body and is
slightly larger than the *pranic* body (*Ka*). The mental body
is slightly larger still because it holds memory holographi-
cally in space around the physical body. From there, the
astral body is actually a subtler sheath that is slightly
larger, just barely larger than the mental body. Beyond
the astral body is the next luminous egg-shaped field
which we call the etheric body. Finally the causal body,
the least dense of all, is a point of light above the other
luminous eggs. All of these subtle bodies emit light and
sound.

These frequencies are too high to be seen or heard

physically, but they can be seen and heard psychically. This is how we ascertain where people are in their evolution—by the quality of the light and the quality of the sound generated from their fields. When operating correctly the sound and light emitted by your fields are harmonious. When you hold a limiting emotional pattern or belief, for example, the colors and sound become disharmonious. In severe cases of self-limitation, one or more of the bodies may actually alter its rotation—wobbling, locking or freezing up—and in extreme cases a subtle body can even fragment.

Virginia: We've been told our energies can go out several feet or more depending on the person. What would you say would be the smallest and greatest size energy field you have seen or experienced to this point?

Hathors: A being such as Jesus or an Avatar will have fields that extend for several miles and in some cases hundreds of miles. In terms of the etheric body of one who has fully ascended, the etheric body includes all of the known universe within itself. So it has expanded to include all levels, all information, all knowledge! Omniscience is available to anyone at that level for they have actually merged their bodies with the universal body. In regards to the smallest-sized field possible, that would be the *Ka's* auric field or *pranic* body during times of illness. In cases of extreme illness, the *Ka's* vitality is lowered and the field shrinks. It can literally pull into the body, so that there is no *pranic* force around, or at the surface of the body at all.

Virginia: Could you describe what the average American citizen going down the street looks like to you, so we have a point of reference?

Hathors: As we perceive humans, they appear to us as swirling luminous egg-shaped fields of light and sound. The physical body can be "seen" through these swirling fields of colored lights and appears to us as a shimmering galaxy of stars. Each atom is like a miniature star emitting a brilliant light, and the organs of your body are like star clusters. When your body is viewed through the swirling fields that surround you, you are quite beautiful. You are to us like faceted diamonds of light, precious and most wondrous. There is, however, something which we find disturbing as we look at your vital force. Many of you are experiencing a decline in the quality of *prana* around and within you. This is a result of many factors, some of which are beyond your control to affect. So it is even more vital that you attend to the nurturance and elevation of your *Ka*. Freeing up your feeling nature will have a positive affect upon your vitality, too, so let's turn our attention here in greater detail.

Now we wish to offer two exercises to allow you to explore your emotional body's nature with greater understanding. The first exercise concerns how the emotional body holds the memory and the energy pattern of a feeling. The second exercise shows how the emotional body responds to a high coherency vibration or the specific feeling we refer to as unconditional acceptance or unconditional love.

৯৯৯৯ SELF-MASTERY EXERCISE #2 ৯৯৯৯
৯ PART A ৯

Let us begin the first exercise by having you sit comfortably or lie down. When you are comfortably settled, recall an emotional response to a particular situation from the past. (For some it may be important or necessary to recall the actual situation so they can retrieve the emotion.) When you have retrieved the emotion, let the situation drop away and then just notice where you sense the energy of the emotion in your body. If you don't sense the energy of the emotion, then you haven't chosen a feeling that is strong enough to create a response in your energy system, in your awareness. Then choose something more volatile—something more obvious, stronger. When you *have identified the emotion, retrieved it, and sensed it, you will be able to feel its location <u>somewhere in your physical body</u>. It would be possible to sense it somewhere in the space around your body also, but for most persons it will usually be somewhere within the physical body. It also moves through the subtle emotional body, but most humans at these beginning stages are not capable of sensing that. They are certainly capable, however, of sensing it as it moves through or pulses through the physical body.*

So be aware of the physical body, sensing whatever that strong emotion is. Sense its pattern–how large the pattern is, the feeling sensation of the energy. Sense the speed at which it is pulsing. Notice whether it is pulsing forward or backward, side to side–whether it is moving, whether it is still. Be aware of all the many emotional characteristics and where they are located in your body. Now we ask that you go back and retrieve another feeling from another situation, a different feeling. As you recall this feeling, notice where in the body it is located, the intensity of the pulsation rate, and where it's moving. Is it pulsating right to left, front to back or the reverse of these? Identify all the different characteristics you can, and specifically notice where in the body the feeling energy is located.

We suggest that you go through this process with various emotions (such as joy, anger, fear, love, peace, etc.) so you can discover precisely *where* in your emotional body you hold these specific patterns. Regrettably, many humans are disconnected from an awareness of their feelings and emotions through childhood training and cultural conditioning. They are not taught to be sensitive to feelings that arise. They are often completely unaware of their feelings and go floating off in their mental body, not aware of the physical sensation that emerges when feelings occur.

This is most unfortunate since they are cutting off a major form of information about themselves and their world. Impulses from the subtle realms of consciousness are received first through the feeling nature, and only later are they interpreted by thought and language. Those who stay "up in their heads" are depriving themselves of a more direct experience of the world and their place in it.

When you are too mental, you can be driven by a feeling that you are not even aware of, and it becomes part of what your psychology calls "the unconscious." This is the antithesis of spiritual evolution. So it is essential to train yourself to be aware that you're having feelings! Equally essential is to notice where these feeling energies move in your body. Where do they pulse? How intense and in what direction is that pulse? For some readers this may be quite elementary, while for some others this is a revolutionary idea. Whether you are advanced or a beginner, awareness is always the first step.

Now Virginia we pause for your questions.

Virginia: Could you say whether positive or more volatile emotions might be the best place to begin?

Hathors: We suggest that you move through many emotions, including what you would term "positive" and "negative," so you can sense where the *negative* emotions pulsate, what they feel like, and then where the *positive* emotions pulsate and what they feel like. The next step in this process, which we will give shortly, deals with positive coherent feelings. The beginning step is to become aware that you have a *vocabulary of emotional responses* which are not a vocal language but do express in the language of pulsation, rhythm, and location when you notice them. Indeed it is possible, by focusing on these pulsations, to receive the information they are attempting to communicate as an aid to joyful, conscious living.

Virginia: Okay, let us better understand pulsation, rhythm, and location. These would probably be difficult for most people to begin to establish without guidance. Have you any suggestions as to how they might best begin? Singularly or in groups?

Hathors: We would suggest each person go back through their memory and choose a strong feeling connected with a situation that evokes an emotion for them. They may wish to start with a positive feeling, but it really doesn't matter. Think of it as a replay of a former experience. Simply recall the situation very clearly as it felt the first time. Bring the feeling to awareness and notice where it is located in your physical body. The location of the feeling in the body is literally where it is pulsating in the emotional body's field. At this location, the energy flows that are within your emotional body interpenetrate the physical body, so where you feel the emotion pulsating is the place where the emotional body's energy is pulsating. Now its message to the physical body can be acknowledged.

Virginia: In describing the emotional body, then, could you indicate what it looks like?

Hathors: We perceive the emotional body as a luminous egg-shaped energy field of suspended particles of light—billions and billions of tiny particles of light. And some of them are very different colors. Some of them are dark, some of them are gray, some of them are very black. Some of them are brilliant white, gold, blue—all the various colors—and they identify where the memory pattern of the emotion or the feeling is located. So that when one experiences despair, for example, there's actually an activation of light particles that hold that emotional memory pattern of despair—that negative response—in place until it is changed. If you experience joy or ecstasy, however, there is another color band that emerges and other particles holding that frequency are activated.

There is a tendency for certain physical body areas to hold particular patterns of emotion. You may experience sadness or joy in the heart area for instance, whereas you might experience *fear or anger through the entire body, especially its periphery.* It varies from person to person, but the exercise is designed to begin to educate you as to how you hold the emotional patterns of memory in your own field. As you're in the daily process of living life, this permits you to have a clearer awareness of your feeling responses to situations.

Virginia: Thank you. Are you saying that there are common patterns of emotion that the human family shares–such as when they are angry, outraged, sad, joyful, loving, etc.? Or are we each so unique that our patterns look totally different?

Hathors: There are some commonalties, but there are many unique patterns that take place within the broad, common pattern. For many humans, the emotions of sadness and grief are experienced in the chest area first, and then in the area of the face–which responds to those heartfelt painful emotions–causing a feeling of "pulling down." People often want to cry when energies are pulling down from the face and the eyes, because that is a release, but the actual pattern of the sadness will often be in the heart and the lung area.

In the same way, the feeling of joy is felt through the heart center. The feeling of compassion is also felt through the heart center. However, *the feeling of ecstasy is a cellular occurrence that permeates the entire body.* What happens in ecstasy and bliss is that the *Ka* begins to vibrate at a very fast rate. The harmonics open in such a way as to stimulate the brain and central nervous system, especially the neurotransmitters, which begin to stimulate the cells into a feeling of ecstasy and bliss. This then becomes a full-body sensation and emanates throughout the entire body in every cell!

This feeling of excitation is distinctly different from the feeling of anger which moves into the peripheral area of the body just under the skin, often moving into the arms or legs, and sometimes causing a desire to hit or to kick.

The feeling of fear or terror is also right below the surface of the skin, and this fear energy engulfs the body from head to toe. It is as if you are totally engulfed in the fear. Which is why, from an energetic standpoint, fear is such a difficult emotion for humans. Since it involves and influences the full body, it can override other processes such as clear thinking. So this is a general view of it. Is there something more specific you're looking for?

Virginia: I've always been advised there are only two four letter words that control our lives. One word is fear and the other is love. Is this similar to what you are describing?

Hathors: Yes, from our understanding we would agree that there is either love or fear in terms of the emotions. One can respond with love or one can respond with fear, so the response is a choice—though this may be difficult to understand. The positive choice of love, for instance, may not seem possible in a difficult moment, because the energy pattern of the emotional body, if it is strong enough, will override the mental body.

Virginia: For example, I've always been frightened of snakes. Now if I see a snake—my first response is fear. I shudder. Yet in this life I have not been bitten or attacked by a snake; so my thought process has clearly been influenced in some negative way.

Hathors: From our understanding, this is the very point. The energetic thing is to realize that the emotional body and the *Ka* are very close. So what happens when fear occurs is that the emotional body begins to vibrate very fast, and, if you identify with the emotion of the fear, then the fear becomes amplified. Depending on how strong the fear pattern is, it may be possible to talk yourself out of feeling fearful. But when the emotional body vibrates in a full-fledged attack of fear, it will override the mental body and you won't be able to think your way out of the situation. You will just be paralyzed with fear.

But, if one goes to the Ka, one can transmute the fear

very quickly. The solution goes back to the central column or *pranic* tube. When you experience an intense, difficult emotion or feeling, first identify where in the body it's located because you'll need that reference point. Then you go to the *Ka*, the *pranic* tube, and hold your awareness in the center of the tube that goes right through the middle of the body. In other words, your awareness shifts to the *Ka*. What will happen is that the emotional body will begin to shift, and as the vibration of fear begins to oscillate with the stability of the *pranic* tube, the fear will become more and more subtle, more manageable.

Virginia: That's very hopeful.

Hathors: As an analogy, consider those toys you call tops which children play with and spin. Tops have a central column of energy–though it's invisible–that runs up through the middle. That's its center of gravity, its center of balance, actually. As long as the top is spinning with enough speed it will stay upright. But as it loses speed, it will start to wobble, become unbalanced and fall over.

That's very similar to the dynamic between the *Ka* and the emotional body when you experience a negative emotional response to something–you can have a feeling that you are literally out of balance, can't you? This happens when the emotional body is spinning and vibrating in a resonance that is out of balance. However, if you locate where that sensation is in the body and at the same time link your awareness to the *pranic* tube, your emotional body will come back into balance very quickly.

Virginia: Then when you feel this fear which is all-encompassing, even as love is, you ask yourself where it is in the body?

Hathors: Yes, that is correct. You recognize the fear everywhere. Then what happens for most humans is that their thinking process panics with thoughts like, "It's overwhelming! There's nothing I can do!" So what we recommend is that you move your awareness in that moment to another part of your energy body. Move it into the *Ka*, move it into the *pranic* tube and be aware at the same time of the *pranic* tube and of the emotion that you're feeling in your body. This way you will find the emotion dissipating or coming into a more balanced state.

Virginia: So you're saying that as long as the *Ka* is strong, it can ameliorate this other situation of fear?

Hathors: That is right.

Virginia: But if the person is not full of good energy at the *Ka* level, then that causes debilitating conditions?

Hathors: Yes.

Virginia: This is why it's critical to feed and maintain our energy level, then, because Christ Jesus once said that humans lose their mastery at the emotional level.

Hathors: That is our experience as well.

Virginia: So it is absolutely vital to keep the *Ka* energy strong?

Hathors: Yes. Attending to the *Ka* on a daily basis becomes part of one's daily life. It is simply part of the human equation for health and higher consciousness.

Virginia: As important as eating?

Hathors: Yes. Understand that the *Ka* is the essential fundamental body. *The Ka can exist—even after the physical body dies—for a certain period of time which can be as much as several thousand years.* Some of the ancient practices in Egypt were to activate the *Ka* so that one survived one's death consciously until one was able to move with full awareness and consciousness up into the higher bodies and realms of awareness.

Your potential is much higher when you develop the *Ka*, because the *Ka* vibrates much faster than any of the bodies—with the exception of the etheric and the causal. The *Ka* supplies the building blocks, if you will, at the subtle realm for the actual physical body, the actual cells. It supplies the energies and the architecture for the mental body and the emotional body and it also sustains the astral body. If you were to remove the *Ka*, those subtle bodies would dissolve. If you were to dissolve the physical body, the mental body and the astral body, but the *Ka* was still strong, the *Ka* would remain. So the *Ka* is like a master over the lower bodies, if you think of it this way.

The other bodies become as servants to the *Ka*, the *pranic* body, and the life-force. Then if one takes that life-force and directs it to the higher bodies in service to the etheric, the causal, the monad, the Source of all that is—then one has a truly powerful alchemy! It is possible to develop the *Ka* without surrender and service to the One Source. But of course that is not our teaching, and that is not what we are here to promote.

Virginia: This explains why some of the beings who were quite attached to earthly matters–through the lower *chakras*–are visible as "ghosts" and "apparitions" after bodily death?

Hathors: Yes, and they really do exist!

Virginia: Is there anything else you would like to say before we go on to the next exercise?

Hathors: We just want to be sure that it is clear to the reader how to use the *Ka* to balance uncomfortable emotion in the way we have just described. The first step is for the reader to begin to sense where they feel different feelings in their physical bodies. The second step is to rebalance that emotional energy by using the *pranic* tube, which we clarified previously in this chapter as a necessary skill.

Virginia: I want to be sure I understand this because there is such confusion among writers about what constitutes feeling and what emotion is. Have you said that a feeling is a *neutral* sensory experience but, once it is judged or influenced by thought, it then takes on a different quality and is called an emotion?

Hathors: Yes. And in one sense it's a semantic difference, but in another sense it's important for us to make this distinction. For instance, when you have a feeling response toward someone with your feeling nature you then might think, "Oh, I love that person, or I appreciate that person, or I have compassion for that person." What has happened is that you have used thought, you have used language, to identify what you were originally feeling as a non-verbal, energetic experience. This labeling, or the very fact that you can say what it is you are feeling, is a phenomenon that must occur in the mental body. The mental body has reflected the energy and then has used language to create a tag for it, so you can recognize what it was that you experienced. Before the mental bodies are fully activated in young children (usually after about seven years of age), and especially before they have language skills–they have all kinds of feelings that move through their beings, but they have no way to know what they are in terms of language. And they do not label them as "good" or "bad" unless they are taught such judgments! The feelings are just part of their experience.

So what we say is that the movement of energy through the emotional body is a positive thing because it is how you are going through the initiatory process of your life. However, the habit of humans to label feeling responses to situations as good, bad, uncomfortable, difficult, and so forth, does not serve them. Contrarily, it often causes them to resist things they find uncomfortable. Now, we are not saying that the process itself of labeling and identifying the feeling patterns is wrong. But we are saying that, if the *result* of labeling causes you to clamp down and prevent yourself from moving through an emotional experience, then that is anti-evolutionary–because it locks-up and "freezes" the energy bodies.

Virginia: Now when you say "freezes," does that mean that the actual vibratory frequency becomes static?

Hathors: It blocks; it stops; it becomes rigid. Then the *Ka* has to respond and tends to get jammed as well, depending on how intense the emotional response is. When the *Ka* freezes up, *prana* does not flow into that area of the body where the emotional pattern is held. So if that emotional pattern tends to be fear and is held in the kidneys, for example, the *prana* cannot flow into the kidneys; and you may eventually have a problem on the physical level with the kidneys.

Virginia: Is there more that you would like to say about this?

Hathors: The second exercise we offer you today is the experiencing of unconditional acceptance and unconditional love, so you can sense what happens in your field, in your body, when you move into this feeling state. Remember that as you move into this feeling state, you begin to set off an inter-cellular resonance that is highly coherent and reinforces the strength of the genetics–the DNA in different levels of the body. The more often you choose to experience unconditional acceptance and the more often you choose to feel unconditional love, the more often you set up a harmonic in the emotional body that is very beneficial and very strengthening to both the *Ka* and to the physical body. This is a basic process that allows you to move faster into the ascending spiral of consciousness.

✨✨✨✨ SELF-MASTERY EXERCISE #2 ✨✨✨✨
✨ PART B ✨

The process is simply to take a moment in the day and recall loving, accepting feelings and then maintain them for two or three minutes. A further help is to intermittently remember those loving feelings throughout the day. Intensify the feelings so the emotional body vibrates with these feelings. Intensify them so that the Ka responds and the physical body will follow. It is a wonderful, pleasurable experience and it strengthens your ability to hold coherent emotion which is crucial as one moves into the higher dimensional spirals. It also helps your DNA.

Virginia: (After pausing to experience the love feeling exercise.) We have a focus right now in the minds of many metaphysical people about their damaged DNA strands. In terms of how you see us as an energy system, could you explain how our energy system and the DNA strands operate?

Hathors: What we would say is that, in your current state, humans are using less than one-third of the genetic information available to them. Of the available codons–which are actual units or molecular gates for memory at the genetic level–most humans are using less than one-third. So there are two-thirds of that unused genetic potential available for use without adding other strands of DNA. In other words, *your present double spiral, the double helix that humans possess, is only one-third activated.* As you begin to move up into the higher spirals of ascension, a need for greater abilities and greater sensitivity develops. So when that need arises, the DNA, in response to the need, will spontaneously open those codons. Then you will find yourself activating more and more of your genetic potential. Therefore, from our perspective, the first step before you even move into other strands of DNA is to fully activate the two strands you have.

Virginia: And these exercises will assist with that happening?

Hathors: Yes.

Virginia: Now, without laying judgment on how this reduction of twelve helix strands down to only two has occurred, is there any comment to be made about people's anger at losing those twelve strands they once had?

Hathors: That anger is wasted for several reasons. First of all, anger is an incoherent emotion and as long as the emotional body holds incoherent emotion, it cannot resonate in the proper manner that allows one to reach the higher spirals. As long as one remains angry about a situation, one is effectively blocking one's growth. In whatever area we are talking about, whether it be on the basic level of one's relationship to other human beings, or the relationship between one's self and one's Creator, anger blocks *growth*. From another standpoint it's wasted energy, because all consciousness flows in cycles and we are coming out of a very dark cycle where consciousness is waking up again. Consciousness itself sleeps and slumbers in different areas of the cosmos at different times.

Sometimes consciousness moves in cycles of high flourishing, but at other times it has cycles of pulling back into darkness, during which potential is minimal. There are points where consciousness, to all intents and purposes, disappears into a deep internal sleep. These cycles last eons and repeat themselves endlessly. It is a cycle of growth that humans cannot even comprehend, because it is so vast. Life is simply the cyclic movement of consciousness and we are all part of this consciousness that is moving now, awakening from its slumber. Our suggestion to those who feel angry about being "ripped off"—as far as their DNA is concerned—is quite simple. Forgive the past! Just let it go. Let the anger dissipate and deal with what is right before you now. Anger will accomplish nothing other than stunting further growth. Embracing love, acceptance and service will do more to heal the past and propel you forward than anything else you can do. One could even use this anger as a part of our Self-Mastery Exercises.

Virginia: Excellent. Do any of the comments or questions I've made during this particular chapter bring forth any other thoughts that you would like to share?

Hathors: No. We feel complete except to say that we encourage you to start practicing the exercises every day. They are easy to do and offer you many rewards. It is not necessary to discard any spiritual practices you are involved with in order to use the methods we have discussed. Our suggestions will only help and enrich your path. Love heals all that it touches, and love opens doors that have been closed.

Chapter 4
The Fear of Opening

Humans, from our experience, are a fascinating group of beings for many reasons. One aspect that we find most intriguing is that what they want most, they fear the most. So opening into a greater reality–greater emotional freedom, greater spiritual awareness–is both a yearning and a fear. This fear of opening to heart love is rooted in many different causes, some of which, quite frankly, develop from how you have been raised as children. In our culture, Hathor children are given a much greater reign of freedom than yours. They are given an understanding of their boundaries, what they are allowed and what they are not allowed; but within those boundaries they are given tremendous freedom. Because many humans have negative experiences imprinted within their emotional and mental bodies during early childhood–when their energies are forced to bend to the will of the adults around them–freedom becomes a source of fear.

We have chosen to communicate our thoughts about the humans' fear of opening to love, because from our perspective the doorway to accelerated evolution and growth lies in what you would call "feelings." We note that as humans open up to deeper feelings there is also a powerful tendency for many people to hold back, to fear that very process of experiencing deep, powerful feelings. So we wish to describe to you how feelings move energetically, how they affect the subtle bodies and offer some suggestions on how to let this process safely unfold. For it is through this process of opening to feeling that your greatest strides in evolution and in awareness will occur.

Please remember that the different subtle bodies resonate to different specific frequencies. As stated earlier, the emotional body is very connected to the *Ka*. The *Ka*, your *pranic* body–the life-force itself–and emotional body are very closely intertwined! If you allow yourself to experience deep feelings, then you are allowing the *Ka* to vibrate at a fast rate. By this we do not mean becoming hysterical, over-volatile, or over-emotional. We simply mean that *the capacity to feel deeply, whether it is expressed or not, allows the Ka to vibrate at a faster rate.*

The organization of the *chakras* is related to what you would call feeling levels. And as the energies move into the heart *chakra*, the "Great Transformer" at the center of the chest, there is a movement of this feeling energy into its greatest tonality or acutely tuned frequencies. The heart area is also the mid-point between the lower and the upper *chakras* which is why many refer to it as the "Great Transformer." It is the Central Sun of the body and it is the cantilever from which all movement takes place energetically into wholeness and into higher states of consciousness. The heart center is "petal-like," but all the different *chakras* literally have an energetic structure in the subtle realm that is much like a flower. Whenever the flower of the heart opens, there is an increase in feelings. So as one experiences more feeling, the petals of the heart open and extend themselves. As one feels less and less emotion–becoming more withdrawn and less attuned to one's own feelings–these petals tend to close up.

Every person has a limit regarding what they are comfortable with in terms of openness and the depth of feeling that they will allow themselves to experience. As we have said, this has to do with their past conditioning. Indeed, your various past experiences have shaped your attitude and your comfort level regarding feelings. What is occurring on this planet now is a rapid increase of experiences in a shorter and shorter duration of time. There are consequently more and more reactions, more emotional and feeling situations than ever before. And these are actually opportunities for accelerated growth! However, if an individual is not comfortable with the feelings they have within themselves and the depth of feelings that can arise, then they may actually attempt to block the process or slow it down. Yet what we would say to you is that this very intensity, this very power of emotion or feeling that you are experiencing in moment-to-moment life, is the food, the fuel, which is moving you into higher states of consciousness.

We have said it before and we will say it again. Because your Earth is moving into a higher consciousness octave, *time is speeding up*. More events and experiences are occurring in shorter durations of time, creating more feelings and more emotional reactions. Understand clearly that these are opportunities for accelerated growth and evolution if you accept them. If you reject the experiences, if you reject your own emotional feeling reactions and polarize them into blame, then you have missed the point. Blaming the situation or someone else for your discomfort is erroneous. Your feelings and emotions are reactions to situations based upon *your interpretation* of the events. They are mirrors that allow you energetically to respond to and become aware of your own calibration to an event or experience. What we mean by this is that fundamentally you are creating your reaction, your experience of an event. Whatever the event is, whatever its ultimate truth is, will elude you until you understand that what you are experiencing in all events is your own projection, interpretation, and creation of it.

For example, if you were to have four people gathered together and something were to occur, you might have four different emotional experiences of the event and each of them would be correct according to each person's perception. There would be four perceptions concerning what seemed to be an objective event. We want to be absolutely clear about this. We are not saying that you are creating the events of your life, although in some cases that is true. What we are saying is that you are creating the attitude about all of the experiences you have that are centered around various events in your life. Your perception of these experiences are based upon your beliefs, your attitudes, your intentions, your hidden agendas, and your feelings about what is occurring.

Feelings give you a very clear barometer, and emotions give you a very clear feedback about what you are honestly experiencing and telling yourself about the experience. If you allow yourself to experience these with openness and acceptance, these deep feelings will create, in you, greater awareness. Simply stated, *the emotion and feeling energies that move through you are fuel for the fires of transmutation.*

Some of the fears of opening to feelings have to do with the actual energetics–for when the subtle bodies begin to open, real physical sensation moves through the physical body. For the uninformed, this can be alarming because one knows and feels that something profound is happening, something earth-shaking! Depending on the individual's personality and the decisions they have made about reality and their place in it, such an opening can actually be terrifying. And yet the opening into the greater space of one's own being, into a greater awareness and a greater sense of freedom and fluidity, is your birthright. This spiritual birthright is what your bodies are evolving to, if you will just allow the process to proceed.

Yes, the fear of opening comes from many levels so complex that we could spend the entire book discussing these complexities. And yet we prefer to be very practical in our sharing rather than discussing all the different complexities of your situation. Consequently, we focus on giving you tools for loosening the emotional stranglehold on your freedom and on your awareness.

Therefore, we now give you a most simple exercise that will allow the heart center to open and permit you to experience a greater depth of feeling. Like all the tools we have given, it may seem deceptively simple, but we have found that the most powerful things in life are often the most simple in nature, the easiest to apply.

ᔥᔥᔥᔥ **SELF-MASTERY EXERCISE #3** ᔥᔥᔥᔥ

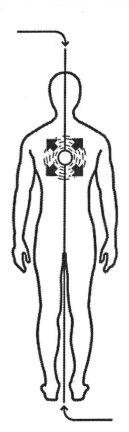

Moving your awareness into the pranic tube, you breathe into the tube as you did in the very first exercise, holding the breath and then exhaling as you allow the prana to move through the physical body. After you have done this for a minute or two, move your awareness into the heart center, the center of the chest–the Great Transformer or Central Sun. Holding your awareness at the heart chakra (center of the chest), breathe in the prana now, both up from the Earth and down from the heavens, letting it circulate through the heart on the exhale. (See Diagram 5)

Continued on next page.

Diagram 5 - The movement of heavenly and Earthly energy into the "*pranic* tube" and into the heart center or *chakra*, opening the heart like a flower.

Merely imagine and feel them begin to move into the heart, for it is not necessary to see. If you visualize a flower opening, that is all right yet that is not the goal, be clear about this. The goal is to feel the energy of the heart opening like petals on a flower and feeling the flower opening larger and larger so that the petals open as wide as your body. Then let the petals extend further and further, as far as you are comfortable in opening. Simply pause and rest with your awareness in this open flower of the heart.

What you are doing in this simple exercise is to activate both the emotional body and the *Ka*. As the emotional body becomes activated, it sets up a resonance with the *pranic* body, the *Ka*, and as you feel the heart opening, you are literally creating an electromagnetic opening in the heart! Once this happens you will feel physical sensations and movements of energy in a gentle way so that your personality can become more accustomed to the feeling of being open. It's simply a matter of becoming accustomed to the feeling of being open-hearted instead of being closed down. As you practice this simple method over a short period of time, you will find your ability to open the heart greatly increasing and your fear of opening greatly decreasing. This is the simplification of something extremely complex.

We hope you will continue to develop the ability to imagine a flower in the center of your chest, its petals opening, because as you imagine the petals of a flower opening like a blossom, the heart center will respond accordingly. You see, there is a connection, an energetic connection, between what is held as an image in the imagination and what happens in the mental and emotional bodies. So as you hold the image of this flower opening in your imagination, in your mind if you will, it is creating a resonance with the subtle structure of what you would call the heart *chakra*, allowing the heart *chakra* to begin to open.

We recommend that you practice this exercise in situations where you feel safe and comfortable, not in situations where you feel uncomfortable or untrusting. Do it with friends or loved ones, with your pets, or do it by yourself in a beautiful natural environment. As you imagine your heart opening, your beautiful flower opening, there'll be a resonance in the heart and you may find yourself experiencing positive feelings more deeply than ever before. Let tears of joy flow, if you feel them, as a recognition of the soul's deep desire to be expressed. Your willingness to allow yourself to grow past fear's limitation is the beginning of wisdom, joy and creativity. Will you dare risk it?

Remember that fundamentally the fear of opening goes back to many levels, but it is ultimately the fear of opening to greater *space*. For as you move into greater space, you simultaneously may feel more vulnerable even though by opening you are more able to receive higher consciousness. Obviously, if you have issues with being seen or being vulnerable, moving into a greater sense of space can be experienced as threatening. But that space holds many treasures. This simple exercise of opening an imaginary flower in the center of the chest can do wonders for any lingering reluctance to open. It can assist you to become more sensitive to feeling your own great depths–and as we have said again and again, "Feeling is the fuel for transmutation and the food for evolution and growth."

Virginia, do you have any questions?

Virginia: Would you care to comment on the emotional influence of prior lifetime experiences upon us? What challenges and opportunities are there for reincarnating humans?

Hathors: The memory patterns held in the emotional body can be carried from lifetime to lifetime, and if someone experienced being shut down or even damaged for being open-hearted, then that pattern will present itself in this life experience. It's important to understand this and to be gentle with yourself around this issue. Also remember that the process of opening does not mean making yourself vulnerable to all who cross your path. It means being discriminating about when to open, and with whom. The goal is to be able to open when one wishes, rather than not having any choice about the matter. What tends to happen with a strong emotional memory pattern is that one feels one has no choice. One will remain closed in order to protect oneself. Through understanding this mechanism, you can begin the process of reopening the heart consciously and then choosing the people and occasions when it is appropriate to expand.

Virginia: So in other words, that choice or discernment is part of the free will process of the human family?

Hathors: Yes.

Virginia: Most of the major religions have talked about the necessity for emotionally walking in our brother's footsteps or moccasins. Jesus was very clear about love and forgiveness; the Buddha was very strong on compassion and the noble path. So, as Hathors, how have you utilized your free will to find safety and balance in this opening the heart process?

Hathors: For us, the essential balance point is the universal stream of love that is literally palpable and flows through all levels of existence. It is a resonance that reflects in our emotion as unconditional acceptance, unconditional love. So it is our desire to achieve this alignment, this balance point, if you will, in all life experiences. Those experiences where we may find it a challenge are our own growth points, just as they are for you. Being in that resonance of acceptance leads one to understand another's suffering, which is compassion.

For us, therefore, the central pivotal point is achieving the vibratory field of high coherency, unconditional love and unconditional acceptance. To live our lives through, and in, that vibratory field allows us to move up the ascending spiral of consciousness. Then we can assist others who may not be in that vibratory field of love, who may not love themselves, or may be actively hurting themselves or another. We have found that being in that vibratory field (love) and experiencing all situations from that positive feeling state has been the greatest catalyst for our own evolution.

Virginia: So by sharing these exercises with humanity, obviously, it would bring joy to you if we could understand and use these processes for our own betterment?

Hathors: That is our hope. And yet we only offer the tools, we don't impose them. From our perspective within that field of love, even if you chose not to use the tools, it does not matter. It does not change our attitude towards you, whether you accept and use the tools or not. We simply know that if you use these tools we have given, your journey will be shorter.

Virginia: Thank you. In your own...I'm not sure civilization or culture are even the proper words...but where you reside in consciousness, do you find individual differences within those that you call Hathors?

Hathors: We are what you would call a bandwidth of frequency, and to be in that bandwidth, we have certain attitudes, certain coherency in emotional patterns. Because if we don't hold a certain coherency we won't be in that vibratory field any longer. So as a culture, as a group of beings, we live in that range. However, there are differences between us. We have differences of opinion, differences of approach and technique, and definite personalities. So it's not all one homogenous custard (...with laughter...)!

We find it amusing that so many think that when they get to the higher levels of consciousness everything is going to be the same. It's not that way.

Virginia: Is there anything else that you would like

to share about yourselves that might help us open our own consciousness?

Hathors: We live in the vibrational frequency of love and joy. We attained that frequency through understanding our own energy systems and by working with these energy systems in some of the ways that we are sharing in this material. We attained this frequency domain quite a long time before humans appeared on Earth in physical form, so we have a long history of attaining and maintaining this frequency realm as a culture–as a "group mind," if you wish. We have a clear appreciation and understanding of the difficulties that are involved in attaining this, which is why we are offering our comments at this time.

Virginia: Would we understand "group mind" to mean hundreds or thousands of beings?

Hathors: There are several million entities, distinct individuals, within our civilization.

Virginia: And if we were to meet Hathors, would we recognize male versus female?

Hathors: In physical form, yes. Like you, we have multiple interpenetrating fields. If our awareness moves into one of the fields and we identify with that field, our energy coalesces into that field. Thus, if we move our awareness into the physicality of our bodies, then we would take on the form that is physically recognizable as Hathor from the Egyptian temple carvings. However, most of the time we do not spend our awareness in that physical field. We spend it with awareness in the higher fields, in which case we would be experienced as luminous bodies of light.

Virginia: So that is why, in earthly language, we would call you ascended? And your success in maintaining this high consciousness has been achieved by the constancy of keeping the heart energy flowing?

Hathors: Yes, that is correct.

Virginia: During your culture's existence, have you had any challenges that were, how shall I say, severe or difficult? If so, how did you overcome them?

Hathors: Our present culture in this dimension stretches back millennia to when we entered your Universe through the portal of Sirius. As a civilization we did experience a difficult challenge as the result of being in your solar system. There once was a planet between Venus and Earth and some of us lived on that planet in physical bodies. That planet blew up and those of us who lived there were killed, meaning that the physical bodies were removed from existence and we had to retreat back to the subtler bodies.

Since at that time we did not have as clear an understanding as we do now about the nature of the subtle realm in this physical Universe, we experienced tremendous grief and loss. Indeed, there was great sadness among us for our lost family and friends. This was a counterpoint to the coherency of love that we had been living in as a civilization for thousands of years. So it tidal-waved us emotionally and took, by Earth measure, several hundred years for us to regain our balance and to understand the experience. But through that grief and through that tragedy we learned something about the fabric of the Universe, something about the nature of the subtle realm, and the continuity of consciousness that we had not understood up to that time.

Perhaps it would help the readers if we describe to them what those discoveries were. The first discovery was about the continuity of consciousness. We knew and understood we had subtle bodies. We had observed that at the moment when one seemingly died and the physical body would begin to move back into its essential elements, there was something that remained at a subtle level—but we couldn't quite get to the subtle level where the beings were still alive. We couldn't make the bridge between our denser reality and that subtle reality where the beings who were once alive were still alive, though now departed from us. What allowed us to understand that continuity was the tragedy of our planet's destruction.

Virginia: Are you referring to Maldek?

Hathors: Yes, Maldek. When that planet was destroyed, it set off such an emotional turmoil that those highly developed ones in our culture, the great empaths and psychics who were what you might term priestesses and priests, had no choice but to go into the depths and track their loved ones. You see, it was a desperation of the heart that drove them past the barriers, past the veils that normally separate different levels of creation. But they tracked their loved ones back and they found them! They knew that they were joyfully alive and that death was not a problem, because the body means nothing in terms of the continuity of consciousness. This understanding was certainly one of the great discoveries that brought a deep sense of peace to our civilization when it was fully understood by everyone.

Virginia: How wonderful! ...I think you said there were several things?

Hathors: Yes, there were several things that we discovered: the continuity of consciousness which has been mentioned and also the connection of the subtle bodies. The relationship of the physical body to the *Ka* was understood at a much deeper and more profound level too, because some of the beings who were destroyed had strong enough *Ka*'s for them to remain at that level in their *pranic* bodies. It was they who were able to actually speak to the priests and priestesses about their experience of being fully in the *Ka* without having physical form. As they dissolved, as their *Ka* began to dissolve, the priests and priestesses were actually able to track them back into subtler realms. So, as a culture, we came to understand about the continuity of consciousness and the relationships of the various subtle bodies, which was actually a great discovery. What felt and looked like a tragedy turned into a tremendous source of richness for our culture. And those beings who seemingly were destroyed, of course,

came back as our children. As so it is with you humans.
Is there anything else?

Virginia: No, beloved souls, but we thank you very much for your energy with Tom today. You've touched me very deeply with your attitude of service and with the information about your own growth and maturity. Again we thank you and look forward to whatever will come forth at a later time.

Chapter 5
The Pyramid of Balance

Imagine a square-based pyramid with the pinnacle, or the capstone of the pyramid, as a symbol of the height of consciousness to which you can evolve—like the one shown here. (See Diagram 6, page 79.) Notice that the pinnacle or height of consciousness is supported by four points or corners, at the base, each of which represents an aspect vital to achieving a balanced higher state of awareness. In your understanding and experience, then, it is crucial that your foundation be secured, that the four-cornered base be stable.

The four points or aspects of this stability which we wish to identify for you are literally the cornerstones of your existence here. Read them carefully, and then note how you feel about each of them.

1. One's relationship to one's physical body and the other subtle bodies including the *Ka*.

2. One's relationships with oneself and others.

3. One's relationship to the service one gives to the Universe, to the world, to one's community—which often takes the form of career, though not always or exclusively.

4. One's conscious relationship with the sacred elements that make up the world in which one lives. For you on Earth these Sacred Elements are: earth, fire, water and air (space).

We have already discussed, to some extent, the relationship between your own physical and subtle energy bodies and the importance of building a strong *Ka*. It is vital, especially now, to secure your physical relationship to the physical body and the other subtle bodies because as your consciousness begins to move upward to higher levels, if the physical body cannot sustain or hold that energy, then you will fall. You will not be able to remain in the heightened states because the body will bring you back. Thus *one of the four foundations of ascension requires that the Ka and all the bodies, including the physical body, be strong and vibrant.* We trust you to grasp the urgency of having a strong and vitalized physical body as part of spiritual clarity and the ascension process.

A *second foundation* is to know oneself and interact harmoniously with others. Regarding one's relationship to other people, you might like to know that in the ancient temples in the mystery schools of Egypt, especially the Egyptian Mystery School of Hator, one was not usually admitted to these schools until one had passed through a certain period of life experience. When people presented themselves for entrance into the school, everything was looked at, including one's relationships. For if human relationships are not established in a certain positive way, then as one begins to move upward in consciousness, negative relationships become an impediment and the initiate will actually fall back down into lower energy states and frequencies.

Today, on Earth, there are beliefs among some people that relationships are superfluous, that they are not really needed, and that positive interaction and relationships with other humans can be bypassed. From our understanding, this belief is in error. What is required is to relate to other humans in a clear, honest fashion so that one is truthful about one's experience, truthful about one's needs and desires, and is communicating these things freely.

The way consciousness expresses itself through relationships allows one to have a powerful mirror that reflects back one's unresolved places. It is easy to delude

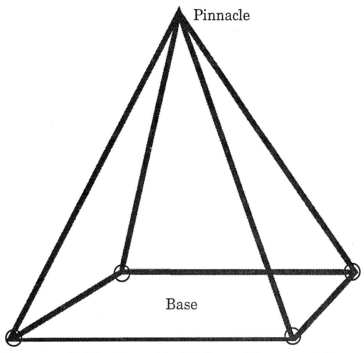

Diagram 6 - The Pyramid of Balance (the pyramid has a square base). ◯ represents the four base-points or aspects of stability.

oneself into believing that one has attained a certain level of awareness and compassion when one does not interact with other humans. But as soon as one chooses to interact, if one is honest and clearly aware, then those places in oneself that are not loving, are not compassionate, will come clearly into one's awareness. Why? Because the other person or persons will "rub you the wrong way." So relating can create friction and considerable un-comfortableness, even pain. It is our observation that most humans avoid these uncomfortable situations by aban-doning themselves emotionally, by not speaking their truth, and by hiding their true intentions from both them-selves and others. Then what happens is, that in that moment of opportunity where awareness could have become crystalline and clear, it becomes muddied and unclear. Unfortunately, this is a condition that is frequently experienced in relationships.

There are many reasons why this imbalance occurs, but without going into all the various reasons we offer you a solution. The essence of our solution is that in relationship with other humans, strive to be more direct, more honest, more truthful with yourself about your needs and desires, and then communicate those more clearly to others. Many teachers on Earth, and from the higher realms, have spoken about the importance of relationships for thousands of years. We simply join with them in emphasizing this truth. When you can incorporate this second of the four base points of your ascension pyramid, the pyramid becomes more secure, solid. It becomes a support that allows you one more level of reaching up towards the top of the pyramid to higher states of awareness and consciousness.

The *third base-point of the pyramid* has to do with how you spend your time on Earth—your work in the world, your service to others. For most people this is your career, although it may not be exclusively your career. It may be other things you do as well. It is how you engage the world, how you meet the world, and what you give the world in terms of your energies, your focus, your service. Your work or service is how you express your true self. There is a phrase…"Work is love made manifest." We are in agreement with this. The work that you engage in is a way for you to manifest your love, your awareness, your consciousness, your mastery. It reflects back to you your personal expression and the places in yourself that are not clear, the places in yourself where you are muddled or chaotic. So if you find yourself unfulfilled by your work, unfulfilled by the way in which you are engaging the world through expressing your creativity and love, then we suggest that you look to those places in yourself where you are unclear about your intentions in that realm. The problem is not with work. The problem is how one engages, or resists engaging, the world through the energy usage called work or service.

The *fourth and final base-point of the pyramid* is one's conscious relationship to the elements–the Sacred Four. Although we will speak more about this later, we shall simply say here that the elements that make up the Earth are earth, fire, water, and air (space). We are speaking here of the elements in terms of their subtle state as metaphor, not in the elements as you understand them in chemistry. These Sacred Elements are actually great conscious beings which may be a new understanding for some people.

The element of air that moves around you and through your body is conscious. The air that you breathe (the space that you move through) is a conscious being. The earth element that supports you, and is actually comprising your body, is conscious. The waters of the earth, the waters that move through the sky in the form of clouds, and the waters of your body are conscious. The fire element is conscious as well.

What has happened at this plane of existence is truly a miracle. For these four beings, these vast beings of earth, fire, water, and air (space), have joined together to allow you to have a physical body form. It is a gift that is given freely so you might have the benefit of experience in a denser world than from where you come. Without these conscious beings' work and mutual cooperation, under the creative desire for your existence here, there would be no evolution possible on this three-dimensional plane. In fact, there wouldn't be a physical plane at all!

Forming a relationship of gratitude towards these beings begins to create a more cosmic and universal understanding of the Creator's energy at a local level. One does not abuse the world one lives in when one recognizes the sacredness of these beings that allow your world to exist. It is out of their compassion, their love and their service that you are able to evolve. For they, like all beings, have the four-based-pyramid of balance in themselves. Their work and their service is to provide a continuity of existence in this realm so the elements are balanced and the physical world continues. That is their work, that is their service, that is their devotion and their dedication. They evolve through this service to you and to all other kingdoms in this realm, in this dimension. You are the beneficiary. However, generally speaking, in these modern times, humans are now disconnected from the ancient understanding of the sacredness of these elements, the sacredness of the Earth.

Your indigenous people are the ones who still hold this knowledge in their tribal understanding. But for the most part, the modern technologically-oriented human has been separated from this truth. So many people wander through the world searching for something called peace, agitated because they cannot find a place to rest. The modern consciousness that has become technologically-oriented continues to create new technologies, ever hoping that these new advances will give one that place of rest and peace. Yet it does not happen. The irony and tragedy of this is that the place of rest is here right now. It surrounds you. It comprises the elements of your body. If you will but see and feel the sacredness of the Earth and of your body, you will find that place of rest. From there you can begin the ascending process, moving closer to the Creative One you call God.

As we have shared, there are four positions that form the base of the consciousness pyramid that allows one to move into spiritual awareness with stability. There are some methods that allow one to bypass these four positions and move very rapidly to the higher states of consciousness and awareness. However, one cannot sustain them until a secure foundation is formed–and a person who bypasses building a foundation will only fall back into lower frequencies. Without the necessary foundation, the higher states cannot be maintained. Since our wish is to assist you to move upward in a way that is balanced and permanent, we recommend that it is best to diligently attend to the four foundation points of one's life.

Attending to The Four Foundation Points

1. *Nurture and strengthen the physical body and your relationship to it.*

2. *Become aware of and strengthen your relationship to your own truth and to your truthfulness with others.*

3. *Strengthen your relationship to your work and to the opportunities for service.*

4. *Strengthen your relationship to the Sacred Elements that comprise your physical body and the entire Earth plane's reality.*

As you strengthen and track these four areas, acknowledging them every day, being consciously aware of them and doing your best to make each of them strong, you will secure the necessary energy that will facilitate a secure foundation upon which you can safely move upward to the higher realms.

And now, do you have any questions, Virginia?

Virginia: I do have one about the four elements. Is there a relationship between what we call the elements and the archangels? For example, Archangel Michael and fire? Or devas and fire?

Hathors: Archangel Michael is connected with fire but an "etheric fire" which is a different kind of fire than the element of fire that comprises this earth plane. The term deva, that is familiar to many, has to do with the beings that move through the earth plane and are associated with different aspects like the growth of plants, etc. There are devic forces throughout creation. There are many, many devas. There is also a devic consciousness that you could use to describe the consciousness of these four elements. So there is a devic consciousness that is fire. There is a devic consciousness that is water. And so forth.

In the Hathor culture we have sound names for these which we will explain when we talk about the Sacred Elements. Just briefly, however, the sound name for fire is KA. It is definitely related to the *Ka*, the *pranic* body that interpenetrates and surrounds the physical body. EL is earth. LEEM is water, OM is air and space. These are sound names given to consciousnesses that exist independent of the names. Fire is a conscious being. Any spark of fire—a campfire, a match, a flame, a candle burning in a cathedral, the fire that burns and metabolizes the food in your body, the fire of the Sun—are all the same being in different manifested forms. So it is with the other elements.

Virginia: How can our present scientific thinking expand to include these concepts as more than just their chemical nature?

Hathors: We have been referring to a different level of consciousness than what you would call the elements of the periodic table, which are the molecular building blocks, the atomic structures for matter. This atomic description of the elements is accurate, but as one moves into the subtler realms of consciousness you will find that things become more metaphorical.

Let's take a journey together to clarify this. When you pick up a rock lying on the surface of the planet, you are paradoxically using the Earth to pick up earth because your physical body literally is the Earth in a temporary standing wave pattern. Indeed, all the silicas, calciums and carbons that make up the physical body come from the Earth. So in a sense it is the Earth herself that is picking up a part of itself in the form of a rock. If you were able to go into the structure of that rock, or the structure of your body, you could study portions of the atomic table and note the various chemical elements that make up both the rock and the physical body. This is at the simplest level of the molecular and atomic structures. If you were to go deeper into the atomic structure, you would open up into something that is pre-atomic, something that your physics calls the quantum field. Out of this quantum field, which is still greatly misunderstood, the actual atoms and subatomic particles emerge. As these atomic structures join, you have the molecules and elements in the Periodic Chart of the Elements well known to your chemistry.

If you move deeper into the quantum field, subtler and subtler, you reach a point where you are in consciousness itself. For the foundation, the actual reality of the quantum field, will soon be discovered as consciousness. So the physical elements are but an out-picturing from consciousness at the subtlest, deepest level into matter. As one moves into deeper or subtler strata of consciousness, one makes contact with what the ancients recognized as the Four Sacred Elements. These, too, are held in consciousness. They are concepts but not mere mental concepts. They are alive! When you get to this level your language is extremely limited.

Consider the possibility that the element of fire is a conscious being–a "field of intelligence" might be a more accurate description. This field of intelligence resides in the subtlest realms of matter, that boundary world where consciousness births itself into physicality. From this "underworld of matter," this intelligence extends into the physical world as the process of oxidation.

When the conditions are right, there is a spontaneous arising of fire through the interaction of oxygen, heat and that which burns (the fuel). Your science is very clear about chemical events that lead to combustion, but there is, as yet, no understanding of what happens at the quantum realm or what we refer to as the underworld of matter. The ancients understood this underworld of matter even though they lacked your sophisticated understanding of the chemical processes involved. Nevertheless, as a result of contacting the deeper layers of consciousness through trance and meditative states, the seers of times past learned how to approach the Four Sacred Elements of earth, fire, water and air (space) as living consciousnesses. That is why in the early days of this planet these elements were actually worshipped as deities. Does that address your question?

Virginia: Thank you. Now could you clarify your understanding of the word "consciousness?" In our western languages this word seems vague at best!

Hathors: Let us first approach this subject using the Hermetic proposition, "As above, so below." This simply means that any level of consciousness will recapitulate or reflect those levels above it and below it. It is simply a matter of scope or dimension. If you look at the human nervous system, you can see that it has the possibility of self-consciousness. Therefore, humans are not only aware of their environment but in certain states of mind they are aware that they are aware of their environment. This is self-reflection, self-awareness. From a physical standpoint this is made possible because the brain is organized so that it can neurologically reference back to itself. This is self-consciousness. When one is awake or aware of what is happening around oneself, one would say one is "conscious."

However, we would say to you that as a human, you are generally aware of less than *one percent* of perceptual reality. This happens because the brain filters out most of what you perceive according to what you expect to perceive, and also because your five senses only provide a very narrow frequency bandwidth of light, sound, and other energy realities. Within that narrow frequency bandwidth, there is a rich world to be discovered and explored, of course. It is, however, only a tiny percentage of what is actually there. If you were to sit in your chair in your room while reading this book, you would be aware of what is happening in the room and also aware of what is going on in your mind as you read these words. But you would probably not be aware of what is happening a hundred miles away from you because your nervous system does not extend that far. Your five senses are reporting from a very localized place.

There are states of consciousness that you can enter and experience, though, that yogis and the ancients have explored extensively. It is possible, as your western science is already beginning to verify, that in certain states of consciousness a person sitting in a room can become aware of what is happening hundreds of miles away. This phenomena is called "remote viewing" and is possible due to the existence of the subtle nervous system. The physical nervous system (brain, spinal cord, and peripheral nerves) senses highly restricted bandwidths of sensory information, while the subtle nervous system is less bound by the physical nervous system and thus is closer to the quantum field of consciousness itself. As this subtle nervous system becomes more developed, awareness can extend into the quantum field, where it is possible to "pull" information to yourself that is non-local, meaning beyond where you are physically located. The impressions are received in the brain as with the physical nervous system, but the source of the impressions is not sensory as most people think of such things.

As you move deeper and deeper into consciousness, you become more non-localized, more connected to a greater realm of awareness. So that finally, at the deepest levels of consciousness, you are aware of all things. This is called being omniscient. It is possible. It is a potential for humans to reach this state. Of course, at that point, you would hardly be human, by human standards today, but you could still have a physical form. Even in your limited historical records, there are reports about beings who have attained various degrees of omniscience, or consciousness of all Creation, through entering the deepest, subtlest state of consciousness. However, unless you finally move awareness beyond your physical senses, omniscience is impossible. It is a matter of scope.

Virginia: I'm not clear what you mean by scope.

Hathors: Scope means the territory that one is aware of. If you are focused on the words of this page, for instance, you will not be aware of your surroundings. If, however, you were to look around you, your scope would change and you would see things that you were not aware of before. Consciousness is like this, as well. If your focus is only the five senses, then that is what you will sense. If, however, you develop your subtle nervous system as well, you will also begin to sense other levels of awareness. These other levels of awareness have been and will always be. They are a part of the fabric or underpinnings of the Universe. But when your primary focus is the five senses, these subtle impressions are eclipsed. The principle of scope, then, refers to which frequency domain you are attending to—where you put your attention, in other words.

In terms of consciousness, the laws are very clear. The principle of scope determines what you are potentially aware of. If you expand the scope of your conscious awareness, then you will be able to enter the subtle realms of consciousness, the bedrock from which all things emerge into existence. If you do not expand your scope or focus, you cannot enter the subtle realms.

Virginia: Is this why we need help and instruction?

Hathors: Yes. Those beings, humans included, who are saints of the various traditions, have attained a certain level of knowledge and practice. They have been able to find that passageway into the deepest self. Because they have done this, they hold its energy vibration. Being in their presence, or learning from them, you can more easily enter higher consciousness domains.

Virginia: Thank you very much. Speaking of help and instruction, have you any advice to assist us in communing with the Sacred Elements so that we may truly appreciate them? Indigenous peoples do this, but for those of us with our western mindset and indoor environment, the task seems enormous.

Hathors: When we get to the section on the Sacred Elements, we will make some suggestions about this. Generally speaking, however, we will comment that people in modern societies do tend to isolate themselves from the elements. They seal themselves hermetically in houses, in rooms where the air does not often enter, where the temperature is kept within a narrow range. We are not saying there is anything wrong with comfort, but we are saying if you live in a continual state of cutting yourself off from interaction with the elements, then you cannot form a relationship with them. So our suggestion would be to get outside more often.

Virginia: Is there any helpful comment you could make to clarify how we might address the levels of consciousness as they relate to God?

Hathors: God does everything. That is the mystery of it. In our understanding, the Source or the Creator is non-dual, neither male or female. We believe that this Ultimate Source set into motion multiple vibratory fields that manifested into the different worlds and into the different dimensions. Those vibratory fields still continue on because if they were not vibrating according to the will of the One, everything would cease to exist. Therefore, it is through the grace of God that everything continues.

Within those vibratory fields, many different consciousnesses have emerged. Those consciousnesses are at various levels and have free will according to the grace of the One. Within those realms where many different life forms have their being, they are able to act according to free will. Again, the quotation "As above, so below" explains the mirror of the creative process of the One. In this process, all the beings that are consciously aware, through the grace of the One, have free will and are able to create in a similar fashion as the One.

Nothing can be done without the power of God because the power of the One is what sustains, creates and continues all realms. Yet one has free will to do certain types of actions within whatever level one has achieved or entered. Ultimately it is God that does it all. However, within each realm where beings have choice, they experience the results of their creation, whether it be positive or negative. One must experience the results of one's own creation. That is what is happening to you within the Earth realm. Humans have the opportunity to experience the results of their creations through the alignment of thought, feeling and their life-force–which is related to the *Ka*.

Virginia: So are you saying that the *Ka* is God energy at our level of creation?

Hathors: Yes. In our understanding there is an Ultimate Source, a Creator, which creates the actual vibratory fields that sustain the entire cosmos on all levels and all dimensions. Within that awesome creation there are an infinite number of lesser creators who manifest worlds, even universes. These less powerful gods also have free will and choice. And so it continues unabated, eternal. All beings who exist and who have self-consciousness are also creators. Consciousness, as it moves into expression within the subtle realms and into the three-dimensional Earth becomes *pranic* energy, or life-force, which in turn is circulated through your *Ka*. As you treasure and protect the *Ka*, you are treasuring and protecting a most precious gift from the Creator.

Virginia: Thank you very much.

Chapter 6
The Ascending Spiral

The Ascending Spiral is a term we use to describe the process of consciously moving upward in consciousness. As you begin this process of moving upward along the spiral, your body, your relationships, and your ways of serving are all elevated. Even the elements that comprise your physical body are elevated. In our understanding, everything is elevated, not just the mind.

As you begin to move upward, you can mark your own progress based on observation of the changes occurring in your four "cornerstone" relationships (i.e., the relationship to your body, to others, to your service, and to the Sacred Elements). Your relationship to others is especially helpful as a barometer of your progress. Ask yourself, "What is happening in my realm of relationships? Are they truthful and meaningful?" The elevation and clarity of your relationships will tell you–in a very obvious and direct manner–where you are along the spiral.

If you feel, for instance, that you are very evolved and yet your relationships are difficult and a source of trouble and disharmony, then you can be assured that you are deluded (...with humor...). We have noticed that there are some humans who go into what they call "the ascension process" and then proceed to cut themselves off from personal relationships and the learning opportunities they offer. What we would say to them is that they have cut off a most powerful mirror, a most powerful feedback process, capable of telling them whether or not they are ascending or are simply deluding themselves. There is a great danger of self-delusion in the process of ascension.

Self-delusion can actually increase on the path of ascension due to something called "spiritual ego." As one traverses the upward spiral there will be an increase in one's abilities and powers. If unchecked, the spiritual ego tends to become smug and self-inflated. This lack of discernment and humility is dangerous. Why? Because you will fall from the elevated states of awareness if you look at others with disdain and separation. So the spiritual ego can be a very real problem that emerges as one starts the process of moving upward, and this is why relationships are also such an important part of the process.

In ancient Egypt, people who were not psychologically or socially balanced, would not be admitted to the Mystery Schools. This was a wise decision because it was too dangerous to activate the higher energies without having the necessary clarity and stability. To understand the ascending spiral concept more easily, picture a pyramid of balance with its square base having four base-points and a pinnacle at the top, as you observed in Diagram 6, Chapter 5. Now, picture a spiral starting at any base-point and moving up to the pinnacle (see Diagram 7). Notice that any upward-moving spiral will have a possibility of four movements, one from each base-point.

In fact, the spiral can move upward from any one or all four of the base-points. You can, for instance, enter this spiral process by clarifying and cultivating positive relationships with others. You can enter the ascending spiral through your highest vision of service. You can also enter the spiral by cultivating your own life-force, and you can rise up the spiral by clarifying your relationship to the Sacred Elements of earth, fire, water and air (space).

You have four possible spirals, then, that can move independently or together and, of course, together is the most powerful of all! If you utilize the powerful synergy of four spirals moving upward simultaneously, enormous

Infinity

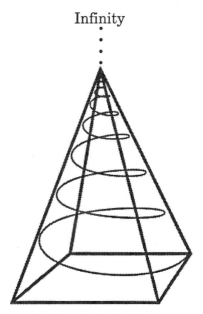

Diagram 7 - The Spiral of Consciousness

growth in consciousness is possible because the ascending spiral is never-ending. *The Spiral of Ascension extends
upward to infinity, and there is no limit to the heights you
can reach.* However, the rate of conscious advancement
using those four aspects within the spiral at any given
time *must be balanced.*

Let's say that you wish to move upward in a balanced
spiral. How would you do that? By reaching the same level
of consciousness and capability in all four areas, simultaneously, omitting none of them. If you elevate the *Ka* and
you elevate your relationships, you elevate your work and
you elevate the elements, then that foundation has moved
up and you're in balance. But if you have developed your
Ka and moved that up...and you have developed accord
with the elements and moved that up...and you've developed your service...but you pay no attention to your
relationships, then you've got a mess (...with laughter...).
Why? Because what should be a balanced plane of

stability is tilted dangerously in one sector. Consequently, when the spiral starts to move up it cannot go any higher because the foundation on that corner of the pyramid is not there. It's missing. It is best to elevate all four positions of the pyramid so your growth can be stable.

The way to conceive of it is to surrender to and become dedicated to the highest possibilities in each of the four areas or situations. Surrender yourself to a vision of the highest situation as you interact with another human and then come from that attitude. In your relationship to your own life-force energy just accept the reality of whatever is happening and work to improve it. If, for instance, you surrender yourself to the possibility of achieving the highest personal energy and health, then you must act in a way to try to bring that possibility into existence by making the right life-style choices.

Thus by surrendering to the highest possibility in *each* of the four areas or situations, all four areas become harmonious. This intention of the highest possibility should balance out the four foundation areas of your life if properly attended to, allowing your frequency shift to occur in balance. Reflecting on and then choosing to grow in these four areas of life is very different from what many humans normally do, however.

The process of moving up the Spiral of Ascension takes energy. It is far easier to simply be in lethargy and unconsciousness, which is the state and the choice of many humans. It takes energy to move up the Spiral and into the higher realms. We know there are some people who say that the path to higher states of consciousness is very easy and it doesn't really take any work, only thought. However, we would say in our experience over millennia that this is not true. It does take effort. Now there is grace along the way that helps, but it still takes effort to move through places that do not wish to change and grow.

What allows you to have that energy to move upwards is the *Ka*. Only with ample *Ka* and ample life-force will you have the power and the strength to clear your thoughts and balance your emotions. You need the energy to successfully interact with someone or you will not even have the possibility of surrendering to the highest vision for that relationship. In fact, without sufficient life-force you will be so depleted that you can barely interact at all. That is why we started with and why we keep reinforcing this basic concept: "You *must* build the *Ka*; you *must* build the life-force!"

As you treasure your life-force, it is natural to also treasure opportunities to relate with people, opportunities to do your life's work, and opportunities to become fully aware of the elements. This combination brings you up the spiral where you achieve a new level of stability and balance. And once you have reached that new level, there's another new level to master. In fact, *there's a non-ending choice regarding how masterful you can be!* We have learned that once you have attained a certain level of self-mastery, a new level opens and you can choose to move up the spiral to that next level, if you wish, *provided you elevate all four aspects of the pyramid of balance.*

Now, Virginia, has our material created any questions in your mind?

Virginia: Related to your description of the four-cornered foundation and the balanced elevation of its spiral, could you be more explicit in describing what's happening at the apex? I'm not sure...

Hathors: Well, the apex always changes and moves.

Virginia: I mean, does the whole composite energy from the four corners up to the apex at the top of the pyramid arise in an ongoing spiral movement?

Hathors: Yes, yes. The pyramid extends. We are using the pyramid as a metaphor to describe something that is not truly this way but is a model to try to communicate something. Using this model...when you have reached the pinnacle of the pyramid this would be a high point of consciousness where you are more aware than you were before of your life-force, of your relationships, of how you are working and serving, and of your relationship to the Sacred Elements. That consciousness increase would be a pinnacle, the high point on the pyramid. However, as you begin to move to that higher level, the pyramid gets larger and extends further upward so that you never reach the end. That's why we can be humble, truly humble, in serving you. Truly, we have learned that the spiral is infinite and there are beings far more developed than we are. So it would be ludicrous for us to judge you. It would be an absurd waste of energy and it would bring us back down the spiral.

Virginia: So you notice but don't judge our faults?

Hathors: Yes, it's just an observation, it's not a judgment.

Virginia: Then in your experience, those in your culture who assist us in some way are expanding into higher awareness on the pyramid?

Hathors: Yes, that is the law of the pyramid. We do this for self-interest, but because you are our brothers and sisters, it is loving self-interest (...laughing...). By serving you we grow. The more awareness, masterfulness, compassion, and love we use to serve you, the higher up the spiral we go, so we all move upward together. There are some people who slide back down, but that's fine because there is free will in the process. Eventually, when someone hits the bottom, that person can still go back up because there's no other ultimate direction (...with much laughter...).

Virginia: So let me be clear. We talk about our personal ascension and also our relationships with others and how obviously vital these relationships are. As people move into spiritual groups, networks, and communities then, because they like and enjoy the energies of other people who have a similar vibratory frequency, does that mean they're being judgmental about those humans from whom they do not feel this frequency vibration?

Hathors: Not necessarily. Spiritual community is a powerful means to help lift oneself up. But let's say that two persons from the community go to the grocery store. If one of them looks at everyone as inferior, thinking: "Look at those people, they're not aware. They're not aware of what we are aware of. We are the chosen ones." That's judgment. That's spiritual ego. And that is dangerous because they are sliding down the Spiral of Ascension instead of rising up.

Another person in the community could go to that store and see clearly that these people are not as aware but hold no judgment about it–perhaps even have compassion and understanding because they have been there before. They would know that in the infinite ascension of the great unending spiral, even their expanding consciousness is limited compared to others beyond them. Truly, there are beings who far, far surpass them, so it is relative. What you create internally, in terms of acceptance and peace, is the critical issue.

Virginia: So during this time of shift and change in the DNA and all these ascension factors you've been discussing, what is the value of being with many other people who open their hearts and minds to greater understanding?

Hathors: There's a harmonic that is set up when people of like-minds and hearts are together, and it reinforces their own vibratory fields in that higher realm. But we would also say that it is valuable to interact with as many other people as possible who don't have that vibratory field. This exchange provides an opportunity to master one's judgment and relate with different energies from a place of stability and balance. And that is what truly will accelerate your evolution more quickly. Interaction with beings who are not of your like-mind can be most instructive.

Virginia: How does this relate to those people who

are energy healers?

Hathors: It's primarily a question of attitude. If the healer channels the healing force or energy without judgment about the person being healed, the "healing" will be pure. If the healer holds judgments about the person being healed as the healing force is channeled, then the "healing" won't be pure. Something of the healer's judgment would be communicated energetically to the one being healed. This would be a disservice, and if a healer cannot suspend his or her judgments, at least during a session, it would be best if the session were canceled. The thought form of judgment can have negative impact even if no words are spoken.

When the one you call Jesus of Nazareth knelt down and washed the feet of his disciples, it was a great lesson. Here we have a master being who brought himself up the Spiral of Ascension so profoundly and to such an elevated level that he could say, "The Father and I are one." Imagine a being of this magnitude getting on his hands and knees to wash the feet of beings who were absolutely unconscious compared to where he was! That is the love teaching, and it was not done out of ego. It was done out of an honoring and a celebration of the essence of those beings; it was done without any judgment. That is the model for an ascended being. A truly ascended being has no trouble washing the feet of those who are less spiritually developed.

Virginia: Yes, and could you indicate how the Spiral of Ascension, based on this four-cornered pyramidic balance, affects the DNA or those qualities we call heredity or genetics?

Hathors: Genetics, heredity–both the physical genetics as well as the emotional effects of family lineage that are held genetically–are all mutable. They can change. And the changing of these patterns comes through an interface among the *Ka*, the emotional body and the physical body. Within the *Ka*, of course, is the life-force, the strength, the power that one can access. If the strength of that power is strong enough and the emotional body holds a particular resonance, a coherency of joy, unconditional acceptance and love, then that resonance moves into the physical body, actually into the DNA patterning, and can change genetics. Your science will see more of this occurring as more humans discover how to surrender to high states of joy, love and acceptance. There'll be some interesting things happening on the genetic level over the next several decades. This will be intriguing to your scientists.

Virginia: There are many scientists already at work on various projects in the United States to understand the composition of DNA and how the little snippets can be used to shift or change genetic diseases. Are there any particular comments to be made about this kind of activity and where it can lead—positively or perhaps not so positively?

Hathors: You mean the discovery of the genetic map?

Virginia: Yes.

Hathors: Well, like all activities of humans, it can go either way. The genetic mapping is an external technology that allows the manipulation of the genetic information, and it is neither good nor bad; it's simply a technology. If one wishes to change genetic structure out of a positive life-affirming desire, then it will become a tool reinforcing life. If it is used to suppress life, to contain life, to manipulate, to adversely control others—that is anti-life, and you have a mess on your hands as a civilization. Given the wide dichotomy of human behavior, it is an area of concern.

Virginia: Yes, thank you. My question, more specifically, is: Can manipulation of physical genetic material afford and provide ascension in consciousness to those people who haven't done the other kinds of things you've discussed?

Hathors: No. That would be spiritual materialism, which is the belief that by splicing genes or ingesting a genetic chemical you can progress without personal growth. The ancient alchemists were involved in this and some of them were deluded into believing that finding a magic potion would transform their consciousness and that they would not have to deal with anything personal. Ah, yes...the magic pill, the magic elixir; and now it's the magic of genetics. *All of consciousness must be elevated.* If one simply focuses on the body and manipulates the energies of the body, there can only be an elevation of awareness of the body, through the body. But if your relationships are not engaged...if your work and service are not engaged...and if the Sacred Elements are not engaged, you will continue to be out of balance.

Virginia: Yes. Then could you comment on some of the current belief systems on the planet related to ascension? We have people here who say that beings that we would call alien or extraterrestrial will come and land or "beam us up." We also may have the possibility of ascension through the photon belt. Those are the two major ones.

Hathors: When we first started this book, we said we are not your saviors; we're not messianic. We wanted to clearly step out of that projection so that the reader understood that we were simply elder brothers and sisters offering our understanding and what we have learned. You may take it or leave it but we offer it freely. In our understanding, the belief that different alien intelligences are going to save you, and the belief that when you enter a photon belt you will magically be transformed, are just projections of human unconsciousness. The hope that someone or something will save you, that you will not have to make any changes in yourself, that you will not have to be responsible, is unrealistic.

The belief that you can stay in patterns of lethargy and unconsciousness, then take something or have something given to you that will transform you without any effort on your part, is sheer folly. It won't happen. Now, there may be alien intelligences that land, for they certainly exist, but those humans who count on others to bring in their ascension and elevation without any work on their part, are going to be very disappointed. *Ascension is a process of self-awareness and mastery on all levels* and it necessitates bringing all those levels of one's existence upward. That is how we see it and that is how we have done it for millennia.

Virginia: Would you care to make a further comment on the photon belt?

Hathors: It's highly overrated in its effects.

Virginia: Are we actually in a relationship with the photon belt?

Hathors: Yes, there are more particles of light but it is not going to have the effect that some people think it's going to have–at least not from our understanding, our science and our perception of it.

Virginia: You would naturally be involved in this whole matter of the solar system entering in relationship with the photon belt, wouldn't you, since you are near Venus?

Hathors: Yes.

Virginia: So you would be looking at the photon belt as potentially helpful?

Hathors: It is helpful, yes, but it will be disturbing to some.

Virginia: Can you be specific what you mean by helpful and disturbing?

Hathors: As you increase the intensity of light, there is an opportunity for the *Ka* to draw in that light and to incorporate that into the physical body and all of its various fields. This can be an impetus to the Spiral of Ascension because you have more energy and more awareness.

Virginia: ...to apply to the four corners of the pyramid?

Hathors: That's correct. Now if a person has not made that decision to move upward along the spiral and to attend to the four corners, then what happens is that the light that comes in can actually be an irritant to the emotional body thus causing a person to act more irrationally and more emotionally. And you will see, as we move into greater intensities of light, that some humans will become more aware, more balanced, and more compassionate while other humans become more irrational, more violent, and more contracted. The light fuels the fire of creation or the fire of destruction. The choice is made within each individual.

Virginia: So in terms of your own scientific interest in the photon experience of acceleration here in the solar system, do you have a timeline for its occurrence? Are there general scientific principles that we could be descriptive about?

Hathors: Yes (...pause...). We're retrieving someone in our group who can explain it to you in terms that are both scientific yet can be understood by your average reader. It's a very complex anomaly (...pause...).

This is how we see it. Everything is harmonic in relationship. There is a harmonic impulse that was set off by the original Source when the Universe came into existence; it is cyclic in nature, and its fundamental harmonic dictates that certain things will tend to move or certain directions will occur at various timelines. This is like the fundamental tone or the fundamental wave, if you will. We have a fundamental wave that was set off by the impulse of creation. Within that fundamental wave each realm is also emitting its own waves. Thus you have waves upon waves of harmonics that tend to bring into existence, or tend to move out of existence, certain phenomena. The photon belt is one of these.

The photon belt allows greater awareness, greater spiritual opportunity. It is simply a door for opportunity. A human may take it or not. A Venusian may take it or not take it, but I guarantee we're all going to take it (...much laughter...)! The door of opportunity is an increased intensity of light. The increase of intensity of light is starting. It's already happening and you can see people losing their emotional balance, people doing irrational and terribly damaging things to each other.

Simultaneously, however–and you don't often see this in your news–miracles are happening. Because most of your news is a source of entertainment emphasizing torture, violence and pain–not joy, service and elevation–you miss the good information to cheer you on. There are wonderful miracles occurring–healings between individuals and remission of illnesses occurring. This is happening worldwide but, in terms of the media, you don't often hear about it on the nightly news.

Not only is the intensity of light increasing because of the photon belt, but the galactic core is emitting high energy particles that your physicists have recently discovered. They are measuring its increase but don't grasp that these particles are seeds for higher states of consciousness. In other words, it's a gifting, if you use that way of looking at it, from the Universe. Here are these energy gifts to move you further along the spiral, if you choose. But if a person has not made the choice to move upward along the spiral and to attend to the pyramid's four basepoints, then these elevating energies actually become a source of disturbance and imbalance. All of us, within this solar system, are clearly going through this process. And as best we can estimate, it will reach an energetic crescendo in the first decade or so of the next millennium, probably by 2020 A.D.

The photons and these particles are actually affecting you–us–and other higher dimensions as well. It's affecting all dimensions in the solar system, not just your third dimension.

Virginia: You mentioned "galactic core." Could you be more specific about what you mean by that?

Hathors: The center of this galaxy.

Virginia: So all physical matter and consciousness

is affected by the photons?

Hathors: Yes.

Virginia: Is there anything further about the time line we should know?

Hathors: Well, it is relative because there are many variables. Therefore, if we give a timeline, you have to realize that this is a *probable* timeline only, as we look at it, since the Universe is always changing. It is not a constant. You can't predict anything for certain, especially now since everything is in a high state of flux or change. However, as we said earlier, the primary harmonic is due to reach what you would call a crescendo, in terms of wave mechanics, 2000 to 2020 A.D.

Virginia: We have Mayan calendars that simply end at 2012 A.D. and also many different reports indicating that there will be many changes around the turn of this century.

Hathors: Yes. The photon belt originates from non-physical hyperspace and is a band of high intensity light particles. As indicated, Earth will be in this belt through the first decade or two of the next millennium, though by that time the effects will have started to diminish. However, as we have said, the photon belt is only one part of what is occurring energetically.

Virginia: Do you feel that your own balanced lives of service will take you to the fifth dimension by that 2020 A.D. time you mentioned? Or how do your own people look toward these processes?

Hathors: Well, there's a wide difference of opinion (...laughter...). We are primarily a practical race and our experience over these millennia has shown us that, in a sense, the theory of "where we're going and when we're going to get there," doesn't matter. What is vital is that we surrender ourselves in love to the highest possibility at each of the four base-points of our own reality, our own pyramid. We will then ascend at a rate that is balanced, both for us individually and as a culture. While there are

Hathors in our civilization who have already gone to higher dimensions, as a civilization we tend to hover around the fourth. But there are those Hathors who have already ascended to higher levels and they work with us and serve us as Jesus served you, because from their exalted point it serves them and their own process.

Virginia: Then as we spiral in the energy of possible ascension, do you see our planet Earth ascending in these timelines you mentioned between now and, roughly, 2020 A.D.? And is it likely that the human family will ascend in large numbers?

Hathors: You're speaking specifically of the transition from three-dimensional space to four-dimensional space?

Virginia: Yes, or beyond, hopefully, someday.

Hathors: We are watching with interest what is occurring on your planet. It is not yet clear to us what the final outcome will be. But it is so interesting and intriguing that we can say to you that beings from other dimensions and other universes are crowding in to this solar system to observe what is happening. It is very, very crowded in this quadrant of the galaxy now because of who is here observing these events. What is getting ready to happen, and is in process, has never quite happened before in this way. There is a possibility we would say, based on our observations up to this point, that Earth as you know her will fully ascend. In that moment, if she chooses to make this ascension, there is a possibility, a very strong possibility, that this will occur within these probable 2000 to 2020 A.D. timelines mentioned.

Those beings, however, who are not prepared or willing to move upward with the Earth will leave and they will find other abodes because it will be a very intense, energetic phenomenon for the entire planet to move up an octave. There will be some beings who also ascend independently whether Earth ascends or not.

However, we wish to share our understanding about

ascension and our bias towards it. To us, it does not matter what happens to the Earth as far as whether she ascends or not, or to humans as to whether they ascend or not...or when...or how it will occur. What is crucial in the present moment is what *choices* each human makes in the four corners of their pyramids with relation to their own ascension. For the ascension process is a never-ending one. *The goal is not to get to a particular octave of consciousness. The goal is to surrender to love and to the highest possibility in each situation that is presented in one's life.* And that serves the whole. That serves the individual in elevating his or her consciousness. Whether they ascend or not, or whether they find themselves dying physically, does not matter. We have observed that this phenomenon of ascension is perceived much like a marathon for some, and they seem to believe that he or she who ascends first is the "winner." This is not our view and we want to be very clear in communicating our bias.

Our belief is based on the successful method that we have developed over the millennia, which affirms that the goal is not merely to ascend to another octave. The goal, as we see it, is to live our lives as fully and as richly as possible, constantly surrendering to the greater power of love and awareness. In living well and acting to create the highest possibility in every corner of our life and experience—our culture, our families, and our communities—our civilization is elevated. Whether we remain in the dimension where we are now, or another, does not matter because in the infinity of the cosmos all of us will ascend.

Our advice, as we approach the next millennium, would be not to concern oneself much with the timetables and phenomena of this time. They will take care of themselves. Besides, they are of such cosmic proportion as to be immune to your thoughts or interventions. It would be far more beneficial to change those things you can, and what you *can* affect is the amount of love you bring to your world.

Chapter 7
Stabilizing in Chaos

Your Earth, as we have previously said, is passing through a monumental and historic time. A time in which energies are fluctuating at rates heretofore never experienced by humanity. It has to do with the passage to a new vibration; and as Earth moves from the old into the new, she is moving from an old way of organizing herself into a new way of organizing herself.

Earth, as we are referring to her now, is a conscious living being. And all human beings must respond to the fluctuation that is occurring as Earth moves upward in her own evolution. You are riding, so to speak, upon Earth's evolutionary thrust upward, and you have chosen to be here at this time so that you could experience these unprecedented changes.

Many of these changes are chaotic in nature, and especially challenging to your emotional body. Consequently, many of you are experiencing greater emotional volatility at the surface of awareness than ever before. This is likely to continue for some time as Earth moves through this transition phase of chaos into a new order. Whenever any system moves from one level of order to a higher level, there is a period of chaos in which perturbation or disturbances are on the increase. This is now occurring on your planet so that all levels–atomic, molecular, biological, geological, social, economic, etc., are in states of flux or change. Of course your own inner reality is affected too, especially your own emotional response to people and things around you.

There are many ways to move into a greater mastery of your emotions during these chaotic times, and we would share with you one particular approach of value. We view you, as we mentioned previously, as a multidimensional energy system. Therefore, what we would share with you is a method to help you deal with your own energy in such a way that your emotional body becomes more stable through this period of tremendous transition.

As described earlier, this method involves moving awareness into the *pranic* tube, the central column that extends from above the head through the central part of the body and down into the Earth. For example, if you find yourself in a difficult situation emotionally, then the immediate shift of your awareness into the *pranic* tube will greatly help. This shift allows the *prana* to move through the *pranic* tube more freely, changing your breath in a way that allows a greater movement of life-force. You will find the emotional body becoming more stable, less volatile; and, from that place of emotional centeredness, you will be able to make better choices for yourself in those difficult moments.

Now we would like to take you through a small series of exercises, as we have done previously, to increase your self-mastery, self-control and understanding.

৵৵৵৵ SELF-MASTERY EXERCISE # 4 ৵৵৵৵
৵ PART A ৵

In this exercise, imagine a tube of light, an energy conduit, extending down through the center of your body all the way to the center of the Earth (see Diagram 8). This is where you are connected, so to speak. Now, in your imagination, allow that tube of light to move upward above the head, as far into space as is appropriate for you at this time. (Some of you will experience the pranic tube going only a short distance above the head, and some of you may experience it going into other dimensions of the Universe. Whatever way and however far it goes above the head does not matter. The distance will be appropriate for you at this time.) With this accomplished, move your awareness into the heart center and allow yourself to breathe with your awareness focused at the heart. As you focus at the heart, imagine and sense celestial energy coming down from above and terrestrial energy coming up from the Earth below so that these two meet in your heart.

Diagram 8 - Balancing emotional energies by connecting "heaven" to "Earth" through the *pranic* tube. This allows the individual to "self-ground" making emotional states easier to manage.

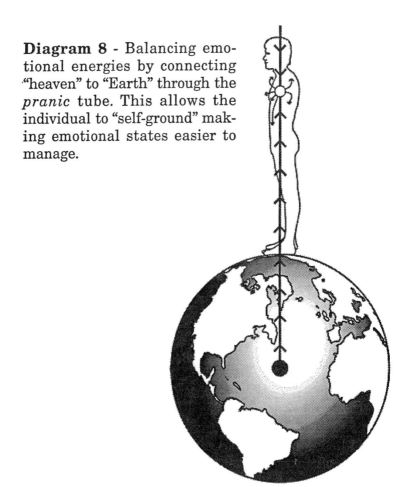

Yes, let these two energies flow into the heart from above...and from below, feeding the heart continuously in a combined stream, whether you are inhaling or exhaling, whether you are pausing your breath or not. Just experience a continual flow of prana moving downward and upward. The goal of this exercise is to get a clearer sense of this flow of energy, of prana, coming down from above and coming up from below. Please pause and take about a minute to get a very clear sense of this flow of prana. This is the first part of the exercise.

❧ PART B ❧

The second part of the exercise does essentially the same thing, except that it adds an additional step. With your awareness in the heart and with the flow of prana coming down from heaven and up from Earth, simultaneously allow your awareness to be on your breath. Now please notice when you <u>inhale</u>...then when you <u>exhale</u>...and also when you <u>pause</u> between breaths. As you become aware of your breath, also be aware of the flow of prana moving downward and into your heart, as well as upward and into your heart. Whether you are breathing or pausing, notice that the pranic flow is continuous. While experiencing that continuous flow of prana into your heart, again become attuned to the rhythm of your inhalation and your exhalation so that you have a sense of two <u>separate</u> flows. Notice the flow of the breath, which pauses and moves, and the flow of prana through the pranic tube which is continuous and does not pause. Do this for about a minute, getting a clear sense of the rhythm of the breath and also a clear sense of the continuous flow of prana through the pranic tube into the heart.

After you have mastered this portion of the exercise and get a clear sense of the continual flow of *prana* into your heart, from above and below, while simultaneously noticing your breathing–then stop a moment to observe that you are experiencing or sensing two vital activities– the rhythm of your breath, for one, and the continuous flow of *prana* through the *pranic* tube, for another. This achievement empowers you to add the third portion of the exercise which uses the continual flow of *prana* while you go through three different breathing patterns.

One is a very rapid breathing pattern, one is a very shallow breathing pattern, and the third merely requires holding the breath. Perhaps you didn't know it, but these are the three primary breathing patterns the breath goes through as you transit through different emotions. As you master holding a continuous flow of *prana* so that it is unaffected by the three different breathing patterns, you will be moving towards greater emotional stability.

✌ PART C ✌

Bring the prana flow down from over your head into the heart, and then up from the Earth into the heart as <u>you breathe a very fast breath</u>. Then take <u>a slow breath</u>. Then go to <u>a pause</u> while holding the breath. Throughout all three patterns, get a clear sense of the continuous flow of prana regardless of which phase your breath is in. Now resume normal breathing. Again, take about a minute or two to practice these three breath phases. As you work with this exercise, you will discover that the prana can freely flow regardless of what breathing pattern you are in. This will allow you to become better stabilized <u>regardless</u> of the breathing pattern or emotional pattern in which you find yourself.

Feel free to stop reading and practice this three-phase breathing pattern until it is familiar. These three steps are your training ground for handling unexpected emergencies and emotionally chaotic circumstances wherever they may occur! When you can feel comfortable with these three phases we can add one more critical step. This fourth portion of the exercise will show you how to shift your focus into the *pranic* tube and ground it into the Earth at a moment's notice!

❧ PART D ❧

Essentially what you do is to immediately move your awareness into the pranic tube of the body (see Diagram 8, page 109) and with your imagination, extend it <u>all the way down into the center of the Earth</u>. As you do this you will feel something pulling at the energy as if it's an anchor, for indeed it is an anchor. Then allow the prana to flow. It is important to understand that by simply allowing the prana above the head to move downward into the heart and upward from the Earth into the heart–and intending it to be deeply anchored in the Earth–you are grounding the pranic tube down into the very core of the Earth. There is nothing else that you need to do. You do not <u>make</u> it happen; you <u>allow</u> it to happen. The prana immediately flows according to your intention. The intention is what is crucial here. The intention of holding the pranic tube anchored in the core of the Earth and allowing the Earth energies to move up, simultaneously, as the celestial energies move down into the heart, stabilizes your emotions. Again we recommend practicing this for a minute or two at a time.

Please pause in your reading and try this exercise now, referring back to our directions as needed (...pause...).

What was your experience like? Did you sense or feel the anchoring? The wisest goal would be to practice these exercises on a regular basis, until you have reached the point of mastery where you are able to shift your awareness into the *pranic* tube upon command. When you can ground it into the core of the Earth, and allow the two streams of *prana* to meet at your heart, mastery of emotion is possible! By allowing the *pranic* stream to be continuous and unfaltering, no matter which breathing patterns or emotional patterns you may be experiencing, you regain emotional control.

So practice this technique in the day-to-day situations in which you find yourself. Use it in situations where you may previously have become frustrated or angry ...situations that may have triggered sadness...situations that brought up fear. Yes, practice this technique and you will create an amazing sense of stability and groundedness in a way you may never have experienced before. From this place of power you have the option of moving into a greater choice of alternative responses to a situation, because you will not be swayed by emotions as in the past.

An example of a practical application may prove helpful here. If you have a problem in a certain area, in a particular level of experience, then one way of solving that problem is to deal with it at the level where the problem exists. Another possibility, however, is to either go below the level of the problem, or to the levels above it, so that you do not deal with the problem *directly*. Rather you deal with it by going to levels above and below it that are not disturbed. This is essentially what you are doing in this technique when you are connecting to the celestial realm of higher vibratory frequency. Similarly, connecting to the terrestrial energies of the Earth that have little to do with human problems, allows these two streams of energy to move into the *pranic* tube, which is their natural flow. You are not doing anything that does not already occur. What you are doing is expanding your awareness to include this energy channel or *pranic* tube.

Being conscious of this energy core that extends through your body creates a way for you to stabilize your subtle bodies, stabilize your magnetic and electro-magnetic fields, and stabilize the emotional body so that you find yourself responding to difficult situations from a place of balance. It will be a remarkable shift for some of you who feel as if you are frequently buffeted by chaotic emotions and your own seesaw reactions to life's situations. Please note that mastery of the emotional body is not the same as the suppression of emotion. The goal is to feel emotion deeply and fully in a balanced and integrated manner. Suppressing (denying) feelings and emotions will not serve you.

For those of you who already feel somewhat emotionally stable and generally unaffected by strong negative emotions in daily living, it is still a very good technique to learn since there are massive changes underway for your planet—and what occurs in one area of the world affects the energetics on the other side. We see your world as one interconnected consciousness, one interconnected energy grid. Therefore, what occurs in Bosnia will affect, energetically, what occurs in New York. What occurs in New York will affect what happens in Mexico, in Africa, and so on. Whenever you have a large-scale energy phenomenon such as many people dying from Earth changes, war or genocide, you will have an electro-magnetic disturbance that moves throughout the entire grid.

If you are able to balance yourself through this method of connecting to the *pranic* tube and allowing the *pranic* flow to be continuous, then you can stabilize yourself in situations that might otherwise throw you off center, so to speak. We realize that we have been quite intense about these exercises, so we trust that you realize their importance. They are such invaluable tools, so very simple and very effective. And yet, in order to master the process, *you must use it.* The exercises have to be *practiced on a regular basis* until you know, beyond a shadow of a doubt, that you have mastered them!

Relatively few humans living in highly technologically developed countries have studied yogic techniques and other meditative practices well enough to claim that they have stable emotional fields under adverse circumstances–which is why we have come forth with this information. We believe these exercises provide a fast, safe way to assist humans to achieve greater consciousness in everyday living. Please try them with personal commitment and persistence until you know they work for you as an *energetic* reality.

And now, Virginia, what are your questions?

Virginia: In this book we are given a number of practical methods or exercises to help us retain stability in our emotional bodies during these challenging Earth times. I'd like to ask where and when these exercises were developed, and did or do Hathors use them today?

Hathors: The exercises were developed in our group for the purpose of giving them as tools to humans at this time. The understanding of the energetics goes back to a fundamental understanding of magnetic fields–a knowledge that was used in the Temple of *Hator*, in Lemuria, in Atlantis, and even prior to that. All human forms have a magnetic field, a North pole and a South pole, and this *pranic* tube or column that runs through the middle of the body. So we developed tools specifically tailored for you at this time. They are offered as tools that may assist you. Today, we Hathors use them automatically; we don't even have to think about it.

Virginia: It's become a way of life?

Hathors: It's become a way of life and energetics for us. It happens as naturally for us as breathing.

Virginia: Do other civilizations use these exercises or practices?

Hathors: They will use something based on the same energetic principles, yes.

Virginia: So in other words, as long as you retain any aspect of an emotional field, some kind of support is necessary.

Hathors: Yes, if you desire to have mastery of the emotional body. Mastery, however, is not the same as control. The goal is not to suppress the emotional body, but to stabilize it. And energetics are definitely a part of this, because Earth reality is very much a school for learning to master one's emotions without suppressing or controlling them. One of the things that beings definitely come to this planet to learn is to ride the energy of emotion in a masterful way.

Virginia: This specific emotional aspect?

Hathors: Yes. It's part of the "curriculum."

Virginia: May we assume that these exercises could not possibly cause any harmful effects to people who use them?

Hathors: Correct. They cannot cause harm if used as described.

Virginia: And since they're safe, would practicing them with a partner have value? Doing them in groups? Or is it better to always practice them alone?

Hathors: It depends on the person's temperament. Some people really can't sustain their practice unless they have a partner or a group. Therefore, it can be done individually, with a partner, or with a group—whatever facilitates it for the individual. The essential thing is to continue to work with it until it becomes an automatic reflex, until it becomes so much a part of you that you do not have to think about what to do in an emotional or chaotic situation. The goal of repetition (practicing) is to reach a point of mastery where emotions can be balanced at a moment's notice.

Virginia: Could you speak about the importance of sound as a preparation for understanding these energies that you bring? I am aware that Tom Kenyon does toning using his wonderful 4 1/2-octave vocal range. Would it help for people to be in one of his seminars first and experience through his voice what these healing sounds are like? Would that also happen through a video or an audio tape?

Hathors: Hearing the sounds and feeling them in person is a superior way to receive the information because more activation occurs when your physical body is in the same space where the sounds are being made. However, just hearing the sounds on either a video or audio tape would have a very powerful and positive effect. We do our work primarily through sound. The cognitive pieces we are giving are less than *one percent* of what we offer, but it's important because not everybody can arrange to be in the same space where these sounds are being made. Hearing the sounds, however, is like putting on a turbocharger (to use your car analogy)–much more energy, much more power and much more speed.

Virginia: Yes. I'd like to inquire whether you have any advice on how we can use sound to help settle a crowd's emotions and chaotic feelings during times of major emergency?

Hathors: There are two levels–one would be audible and one would be inaudible. If the group is coherent enough to understand and accept audible sound as a viable tool, then you can simply go into the space within yourself that is ever unchanging, calm, peaceful, and where the feeling of connectedness and love exists. It may be challenging to find that space yourself while going through a chaotic experience, but it is still there because it's the core of consciousness itself. So you would simply get in touch with that place and then make sounds that express that calming energy. And as people heard those sounds it would register that calming state within them through the law of resonance. If you are in a group or situation where the audible sound is inappropriate, you can make the sounds silently within and then radiate them outward from yourself. It will have a more subtle effect but it will still be a positive one.

Virginia: Now one question that many people are asking today. In the human body, with all its DNA, RNA and different cellular, genetic and hereditary aspects, how can we use sound to stay well during this period of crisis where we have so many degenerative diseases?

Hathors: Well, you've asked a very, very complex question.

Virginia: Yes, I know, and perhaps there is no single answer.

Hathors: The fundamental reason for these degenerative diseases that you're mentioning, as we understand it, is the devitalization of the Earth. At the beginning of time the vitality of the Earth was very strong because of the glaciers, glacial activity, and the grinding and transformation of the rocks into minerals. The waters were highly mineralized, the soil was highly mineralized, and the oxygen level was higher. Your scientists have estimated that the present level of oxygen averages around *18 percent* whereas it was *30 percent* several hundred years ago. With this tremendous decrease in oxygen levels, the amount of *prana* available has also decreased.

And one might ask why this is happening. It is happening for many reasons, but in terms of human behavior it is happening because you are decimating the forests–even the rain forests–and you are polluting the oceans so that the plankton or organisms which produce oxygen in the ocean are stunted. This part of the problem occurs wherever humans are so disconnected from the Earth that they are destroying the very bedrock of their existence. Because most people are running around independently pursuing whatever they are trying to achieve in their personal lives, there is often little cultural appreciation or contemporary understanding of the need to honor the Earth mother. Consequently, there is mass decimation of those fundamental generators of oxygen, as well as a depletion of the mineral reserves through agriculture. So these are the two primary things that cause many of the negative conditions that, as a civilization and as a planet, you are experiencing.

The question of sound is a complex question because there are specific frequencies that will help with specific health problems, and many of your researchers are only now uncovering this therapeutic use of sound. In the coming decades, "sound therapy" is going to be a very big part of your medicine. It is true that you will discover how to use one frequency for this problem and another frequency for that problem, and ultimately you will learn how to use sound to assist and heal those who suffer. But it is equally true that simply learning them and using them will not remove the deeper cause of much disease–which is your disconnection from the Earth itself. This disconnection must be healed. But our answer to the question you're asking–what can an individual do for themselves with sound–is that a person can learn to apply what is called the Law of the Fundamental Tone.

This law states that a Fundamental Tone rules over all other tones in relationship to it. In terms of music, for example, if you pull the damper of the strings of the piano so that all the strings can sound and you strike a note, say the note of "C," then all those C notes that are above and below the note you struck will resonate. They will begin to sound through the Law of Sympathetic Resonance, and this is the Law of the Fundamental Tone. So a Fundamental Tone can set off resonances in other octaves.

What this means, practically speaking, is that an individual can go to the place in their own consciousness where they are healthy, radiant and have the attributes that they desire. By making the sounds from that higher state of consciousness on a regular basis, they can transmute those other conditions in the lower octaves because they have sounded the Fundamental Tone. So if you have an unhealthy situation, a condition to be changed, then you go into the place in your consciousness where you don't have that condition. When you find that place you repeatedly make the sound expressing that positive quality through your own voice. By doing this over and over again, eventually it will have a positive effect–sometimes even an immediately positive effect.

Virginia: Earlier in this chapter, you made the

statement that the volatility of human emotions is likely to continue and surface into our awareness even more than before, as Earth moves through her transitional phase of chaos into a "new order." I wonder if you could describe what that new order is going to be like when we get there, so that we can hold that positive image in our thoughts?

Hathors: The "new order" is a new order of time and space. It is basically an opportunity for individuals to pass through three-dimensional consciousness into four-dimensional consciousness and beyond. What it means occurs on many levels, so we will describe a few of its major attributes. One such attribute is that of instantaneous manifestation. In fact, you can tell you're getting closer to the dimensional shift when the events in your life move faster and faster, and the length of time between the moment you think or say something until the time it happens gets shorter and shorter. Many are already experiencing this.

There will be a new appreciation of the Earth, and the Earth herself will go through a radical change during which she will become more conscious. There will be a global connectedness of beings. It will be as if all of humanity becomes one mind and one consciousness. (We say the words "as if" to indicate that we're using a metaphor, but it will be as if there is just one consciousness operating with many diversities, many parts.) There will indeed be a feeling of direct connection to one another and also to the Earth.

Virginia: So those are two major ways in which we recognize we're getting there? This quick manifestation and being of one mind seem to border on the miraculous.

Hathors: Yes. It's perceived as a miracle by anyone who doesn't understand the principles behind it, but when one understands the laws that hold events together, and one understands the acceleration of time that takes place as one enters into another dimension, then it does not seem to be a miracle. It just seems the way things are.

Virginia: ...perfectly normal? Usual?

Hathors: That's right.

Virginia: During the transformation will the animals and plants be affected in the same way as humans?

Hathors: The same thing will happen to them that happens to humans. The actual atomic activity of their bodies will shift and they will oscillate at a much faster vibratory rate. And there will be a point where they oscillate back and forth between their bodily incarnation and pure energy–which is one of their natures, their true identity. As they enter the subtler realms from their denser physical forms, then the oscillation will most likely accelerate, and at some point they will be their pure energy forms.

Virginia: I'm confused then. If some of them have a group soul, as has been suggested, how does this work?

Hathors: The transition into another dimension as we understand it from our perspective, does not so much involve just the soul as it involves all levels, including the physical body. The soul is affected, yes, and the soul experiences a much greater freedom in the fourth-dimensional reality than it does in the third dimension. Every level of self oscillates, moves, and vibrates faster.

Let us put it this way: In our experience of ourselves with one another we have form; we can touch each other just as humans do. But if you were to try and see us, we would be invisible unless you are clairvoyant and notice our fields of color and light...unless you tune into our specific perception of ourselves. In that case, you would see our forms because what we have done is to actually filter the perception of our energy bodies through our own self-image. Then that's what you would see. But our central nature in our higher dimension, in relationship to your third dimension, vibrates so fast that it is virtually invisible or is just a blur of light to you. It is like the propeller on a plane. When it sits still you can see the prop but when it starts turning you can't see it. It becomes a blur, like a disc. So it is the same in the relationship between the dimensions for animals and plants. As the plants and animals begin to vibrate faster, those who are in the third dimension will not see them anymore. However, those who are in the fourth dimension will see them because the frequency matches.

Virginia: That reminds me...many people have thought going from the third to the fourth dimension was really wonderful and they were excited about it. Then some influential people began to say that we're going to skip the fourth dimension and go right up to the fifth. So now I think there's an expectation people are setting up that the fourth dimension isn't so great. I wonder if you could clarify or comment on this?

Hathors: This is semantics. Well, we do not wish to step on anyone's toes, so let us say it this way. There are many different perceptions of what is going to happen. No one knows for sure because this shift never happened this way before. However, from our experience and understanding, we suspect that most people who make their transition will do it through the fourth. We may be proven wrong but that is our expectation. But as we said, no one knows absolutely. Not even the archangels know exactly how this will turn out.

Virginia: How come?

Hathors: Because there is so much happening so fast and because, in a way, this has never happened before. As we've previously said, there are beings here from many different dimensions and realms observing the situation because it is so unique. But let us say one thing about human anticipation of shifting into higher dimensions. There are some who really believe that by going into the fourth dimension they will leave their problems behind them. They feel this is the solution to life's dilemmas and that, somehow, everything miraculously will be transformed so they won't have to deal with their current issues. These individuals are in for a surprise! Your issues continue with you in consciousness no matter what dimension you go to. It's simply that you work them out in the vibratory field of that dimension. So our advice to people at this time is very simple. Don't focus on what dimension you're going to go to, or even whether the dimensions are shifting. Focus on your capacity to love and to forgive.

Virginia: Do it where you're at?

Hathors: Yes. Do it where you're at.

Virginia: Well, that's fine. Thank you. Did you think of anything else on chaotic conditions and stabilization that you want to mention?

Hathors: Just that people need to become friends with chaos, because there will be more before the system stabilizes.

Virginia: By that comment do you mean asteroids, pole shifts, and/or weather?

Hathors: Everything.

Virginia: Everything? Does anybody know all the details?

Hathors: No, because it is ever-unfolding. The Great Universe unfolds with such novel expressions of energy and consciousness, that even the Consciousness that created this Universe is amazed and intrigued.

Virginia: Again our thanks for this information.

THE HATHOR MATERIAL

Chapter 8
The Sacred Elements

We view the Earth very differently than most humans in Western cultures. Our view is closer to that of the Ancients and your indigenous peoples.

From our perspective, it is not that God created the Earth and the Universe so much as God is the process of creation itself and that God is inherent in the physical matter of the Universe. From our understanding, where you are–God is. Creation is. Indeed, there is no place you can be where God is not. You are a part of God/Creation. It is central to everything. Creation moves through, and is present in, the smallest particle of matter. From this perspective, all of the physical Universe is sacred space. It is a hallowed temple. Many people are presently cut off from or have disconnected themselves from an awareness of Earth. This has to do with a hypnagogic state of consciousness produced by the belief systems of your culture which insist that the physical world is the totality of all experience.

We would say to you that the physical world is only one spectrum of experience, and that the physical world is part of the Divine, not separate from it. In order to experience that consciousness, you must perceive it by having access to the subtler realms of awareness itself. Accessing that subtler realm of consciousness, the archetypal domain in which the Sacred Elements vibrate as living consciousnesses, allows one to sense a greater continuum of consciousness. (This archetypal domain is not the same thing as the archetypes described by your Swiss psychiatrist, Carl Jung. Rather our archetypal reference denotes a "primordial force" that extends through what we could call "the underworld of matter." This is analogous to the "sub-quantum realm"—a theoretical place where consciousness continually re-creates matter. The Four Sacred Elements are part of this ever-continuing process.)

In our world we have sounds for each of these Four Sacred Elements. "EL" is Earth; "KA" is fire; "LEEM" is water; and "OM" is space or air. These four constitute a vibrational continuum. It is possible to chant the sounds of these elements and enter the archetypal realms in which they exist. It is as if these sounds open the door of perception and allow you to move into the resonant field of consciousness where the archetypal realm of the elements are alive. Indeed, entering into that realm and staying there for a while enables you to shift consciousness and perception in such a way that you sense the profundity of the physical world and also its place within the continuum of consciousness.

This is a very powerful practice. Basically you *chant the mantra, "EL-KA-LEEM-OM," no less that four times and always in groups of four*; so you would chant it four times at least. Then you might chant it sixteen times, and so forth. It is a very powerful practice and we often encourage the chant be done 256 times—or four to the fourth power. This gives you time to allow consciousness to settle in and to shift through its various states so it can enter the archetypal realm of the elements. There you perceive directly the aliveness and the continuum of consciousness that expresses through the Earth plane.

It is very powerful to practice this chant outdoors where one can sense the elements directly. It is also a powerful practice to place your awareness within the *pranic* tube or the middle column that extends down through the middle of the body that we have discussed earlier. By holding your awareness in this *pranic* tube and chanting the sounds of the elements, you actually cause the *prana* that moves within the tube to become rarefied, to become enlivened by the sound, and to activate an awakening of the elements within your own body. It is something that must be experienced directly rather than talked about.

Another thing to understand about this chant is that material from the unconscious very often begins to rise up, because consciousness settles into a very deep and profound state. One can experience every state of consciousness, every state of awareness from absolute boredom and fatigue to high states of ecstasy and bliss, including an awareness of one's own "demons," one's own negative emotional material. All of this can be activated as one chants this chant, so it is important to understand that whatever arises while you are chanting is part of the clearing.

By chanting the chant of EL-KA-LEEM-OM a person is, in our understanding, acknowledging the sacredness of the elements, acknowledging the continuum of consciousness from the Source that you may call "God"—through its various subtle levels all the way into the Earth itself. Here in the physical reality, which would be the densest Sacred Element level, one is affirming and acknowledging the Earth as sacred, one's body as sacred, and one's place in the continuum of the consciousness that one may call God as sacred.

It has been said that the body is the temple of God. We agree that your body is a sacred temple for it is the space in which the four consciousnesses of earth, fire, water and air (space) offer themselves to you in service.

We see Earth as a sacred space, an outpicturing of the Sacred Elements of the archetypal realm of consciousness itself. We see Earth being as close to God as any other realm, for the continuum is whole. Whether one experiences oneself as close to divinity or separated from it, has nothing to do with whether one is on Earth, embodied or not. One's view is something that is held in personal consciousness. It is possible to be in deep communion with the Divine, to feel completely at home in consciousness, and still be embodied. It is not necessary to leave Earth in order to go "home," for home is a state of consciousness, a state of connectedness generated from within yourself.

We see a dangerous situation upon the Earth at this time, especially in highly technologically-developed countries. This situation is the separation of oneself from nature and the elements. Modern culture has isolated itself and insulated itself from the natural elements, the natural world. Western society has taken the biblical inscription "to have dominion over nature" to irresponsible heights. Humanity is oppressing nature. Humankind, in the modern world, is not only oppressing nature and the elements but is seriously separated from them and, as a result, has lost much of its connection to the higher continuum of consciousness.

When one is in nature, when one has a relationship to the elements, one is closer to the continuum of consciousness that leads to the archetypal realm...and from there, it is just one step into the Divine. Whether the culture of the modern world will awaken to this and reverse its position is unclear. But as far as your individual consciousness is concerned, you can always form a relationship with the elements. You can form that linkage from your own awareness into the archetypal realm of the elements. Many indigeneous peoples can do this.

We would recommend that you frequently enter into nature and spend time with the natural elements, for they are the outpicturing of the archetypal patterns. Don't insulate yourselves from the air, the Sun (fire) and the other elements. Embrace them. Appreciate them. Allow your awareness and consciousness to become attuned to the Four Sacred Elements. Chant the names of the elements in a state of reverence and an inner world will open up to you far beyond your imagination. As you enter this inner world, the archetypal world of the elements, you will find a place where you are more deeply connected to the natural world around you and you will see the world with new eyes. You will see and clearly understand that the Earth itself is a sacred temple, and wherever you go–God is.

And now, Virginia, do you have some questions?

Virginia: In this chapter and elsewhere you have discussed what the sanctity of Earth implies. So today I'd like to ask you about one comment that probably is my own hang-up, but I was uncomfortable with your remarks that being on Earth "has nothing to do with feeling close to God." I think I was a bit defensive about the word "nothing" because I feel that for me (and possibly other humans) to be among a lot of violence and negativity, while having to constantly release a sense of separation and duality inside myself and in the society, does tend to negatively influence me in a very profound way. Am I mistaken about this?

Hathors: Our statement was intended to reiterate that being close to the creative energy that you call God is a function of resonance and can occur at any level of the Universe and in any dimension whether one is in space, on the moon, on Earth, or in the Void. What determines whether one is connected to, and feels close to, God is an internal thing; therefore, being on Earth need not be a hindrance to it. It's true that the lower race consciousness and vibrations, as you point out, can create difficulties, but we simply wanted to clarify that being on Earth doesn't cancel out "feeling close to God." It's an internal orientation of consciousness that counts.

Virginia: Thank you for acknowledging that to be in a lower race consciousness can tend to interfere with the stability and constancy of that feeling of connectedness.

Hathors: Yes, it can be difficult, very difficult to be in a three-dimensional reality when your senses are falsely reporting who you are. And there can sometimes be a battle between what the physical senses tell you and what your spirit tells you and yearns for. So we do acknowledge that the condition or situation of three-dimensional reality is not easy. We simply wanted to offer the thought that it is possible even in your dimension to be connected to, and feel close to, the Godhead or the Creative Energy.

Virginia: Yes, and I continue with another quote that you made earlier about "home being a state of consciousness"—which is exactly what we're describing here. Yet I must admit that I and many light-workers whom I know have sometimes felt a longing to be somewhere else. It's like a hunger for a more loving place. So in case some of our readers may have had that experience, too, I hoped you might give us some guidelines about how to be more centered here. How can we use sound, or any other resource, to really feel that this is the loving place we want to be, rather than wanting to go off into some other dimension or place where there is less separation?

Hathors: You have asked a very complex question energetically, and one that is very profound. Since it needs to be answered, let us do our best to address this very large question, with several parts. There are the energetics, the issue of being present here, and then there is the question of safety and the emotional vibration of feeling connectedness and love.

Some individuals, in order to cope with the brutality of this dimension, have accessed and identified with other realms of their consciousness which are not related to the third dimension. For these people the *pranic* tube that extends down through the core of the body and into the Earth is literally retracted and pulled up so that it does not make contact with the Earth. In this way they are energetically ungrounded so they are able to float, as it were, and be in what seems to be a safe zone for them. So the first thing that must happen energetically for individuals in this position who wish to ground themselves physically, is to extend the *pranic* tube down deep into the Earth.

Incidentally, we have no judgment as to whether your consciousness is here or not here while you are embodied in flesh. Consciousness can be somewhere else. We simply say that if you wish to be here and participate through your present embodiment in this passage or portal into the next dimension–this transformation that you are going through–*you need to be grounded*. By being grounded you can respond appropriately in your body, your subtle nervous system, your instincts and your superconscious levels to everything in your life. While safety may seem to lie beyond or to be outside of physical groundedness, nothing could be further from the truth. One needs to connect to the Earth. This can be done by extending the *pranic* tube back down into the Earth if it has been retracted. So the first thing is understanding the energetics of your nature.

The second aspect has to do with the vibration of love, of safety. It is, of course, possible for a human consciousness to withdraw and retract into an internal state where love and inner connectedness is experienced. As a human, you have multi-dimensional aspects of consciousness. Therefore, it is possible to shift your awareness into an internal dimension of love and safety while being unconnected to the Earth (i.e., ungrounded). Then one floats in one's bubble, to use that metaphor. What we hope is that more and more of you will choose to ground yourselves rather than simply retracting into your internal world. By grounding yourself and extending love outward to others, you benefit everyone, including yourself.

Virginia: Thank you. I think your comments clarify patterns through which some of us may have sought the sanctuary of peace. Earlier you spoke about the importance of the Four Sacred Elements. Can you say anything about why the idea of the Four Sacred Elements may strike some people as going back to primitiveness and how to refute that idea, if it is advisable?

Hathors: In a way, it is going back to the primitive, but there is nothing wrong with the primitive. The primitive is the root from which consciousness springs, and human consciousness has become so disconnected from its own roots that you could easily devastate your own planet. So we recommend that you become more aware of your biological rootedness and your connection to other life-forms on this planet.

The fundamental understanding in many primitive or indigenous cultures is that the natural world is "alive," meaning conscious. So describing this aliveness as the deeper archetypal level of the four elements of earth, fire, water and air (space)–may be a helpful concept since at a subtle energy level of consciousness these elements do exist! They're like archetypes for the elements that you would call the Periodic Table.

We are not saying that the elements of the Periodic Table are superfluous. They give a description of the physical elements in this dimension. What we are clarifying is that in the subtler realm that holds or feeds into this third dimension, there are archetypal realms where the Four Sacred Elements are "alive." To modern man this seems like a quaint idea, but there is a profound truth here.

The natural world consists of many interconnected fields of energy. These fields are conscious in that they respond with intelligence to changes in and around them. Thus, mist, for example, can be viewed at the chemical level merely as water vapor, but this is only one aspect. Some types of mist are actually conscious ephemeral beings and one can, if one understands how, actually communicate with them. This communication, by the way, is done through the feeling nature and not through language.

Virginia: Could the word "foundational" or something that sounds more contemporary be used, rather than "primitive" which implies something less desirable?

Hathors: Yes. One could use another term. However, remember that when you become so sophisticated as a culture, as a civilization, that you have sophistication levels upon sophistication and further abstractions upon abstractions, you get so far into the mental realm that you are not connected to the biological reality of your existence. What we say is that the *biological* level of your existence is the taproot by which consciousness is flowing into and expressing itself in this domain...not the mental. And the biological is primitive, basic.

Perhaps it would be helpful to recall that biological experience of physical birth as a metaphor. Recall that within the woman's body is the seed of a child, and before it is fertilized that seed holds within itself the potential for a physical human. If you go down into the egg itself and you look at the genetic information as held in the DNA codes, you would see what we would call the subtle level of biology. This is very basic, primitive and essential, is it not?

As you go subtler into the atomic matrix that holds that together, and subtler still–meaning smaller and smaller–you get to a domain where you enter pure consciousness–for consciousness and matter are the same thing. They are simply different vibratory rates. In consciousness, just prior to that beginning level of the atomic structure, is held a blueprint for the genetics–for the potential of a human in some future time. So that is the archetypal realm about which we spoke earlier. Within that archetypal realm are powerful energies that become the atomic forces known to your physics.

Virginia: So you're saying that these energies are a dimensional blueprint?

Hathors: Yes. Yes. The Sacred Elements are an archetypal dimensional blueprint for the unfolding of consciousness into matter in the form of the elements.

Virginia: I thank you. Can you describe in a simple way how what we call our weather relates to these Four

Sacred Elements and what's currently happening?

Hathors: Weather patterns are a complex interaction between physical forces such as heat, temperature, moisture, dryness, and pressure; so they are phenomena related to the subtle realm of the Four Elements and also to the level where it interconnects with consciousness and emotion. Very simply put, your weather patterns are an outpicturing of your own emotional and mental life. This may seem odd to those who look at it totally three-dimensionally, but from other dimensions it's very clear that when tornadoes and hurricanes move through causing an increase of violent weather, they are an outpicturing of human consciousness interfacing with planetary consciousness and all other consciousnesses on this planet, including plant and animal. If you look at the flow of violent weather patterns, it is on the increase and this is part of the chaos that is occurring as the entire planetary system, including humans, oscillates at faster frequencies. Emotions are then more volatile and this affects what might be called the biosphere–the place where consciousness and biology meet.

Virginia: Then why is it that certain regions on the planet tend to keep these patterns of tornadoes and hurricanes?

Hathors: It has to do with the grid of the planet in those specific regions. Where a particular region has more of one element than another, that element will predominate and create weather patterns unique to it. But as you look at the weather patterns today, you'll see that some tornadoes are occurring where they have not occurred traditionally.

Virginia: So there is some shifting?

Hathors: Definitely there is shifting.

Virginia: Then are you saying that the elements are responsible for the Earth's pole shifts that seem to go through certain cycles every so many thousands of years? And are you also saying that the elements are responding to this human chaos, and that's what could likely cause a pole shift?

Hathors: No. The pole shift is something else. Pole shift is caused by a cyclic pattern with a deeper pattern of consciousness. What we're saying is that many of the weather disturbances that are being experienced are the result of disturbed consciousness at the human level as it interacts with the Earth.

Virginia: Since deeper cycles do exist that have precedence over human consciousness and weather, what are they?

Hathors: They are cosmic rhythms.

Virginia: And what would we call them?

Hathors: We might call it the rhythm of the Sun, the rhythm of the Earth star.

Virginia: So are things such as volcanoes, earthquakes, tornadoes and hurricanes any part of the higher rhythms?

Hathors: Yes. They can be. However, they are not autonomous levels because they're interconnected.

These grids (and we're not talking about the grid established by the pyramids, but a different grid, an earlier Earth-consciousness grid) tend to determine where the mountains will form, where the valleys will form, where the oceans will form. Then the land masses tend to swirl about these grid lines. The grid lines are sensitive to the greater cosmic rhythms of the Sun and other celestial forces. Consequently, when something gets triggered, say in the Sun, it can set off a resonant effect in both the magnetic lines and the non-magnetic grid lines that run through different areas, such as the Pacific Rim. Then you can suddenly get an increase of volcanic activity. We expect your scientists will shortly uncover that there is a more profound relationship between movements of energy in the Sun and what happens on the Earth than they realized.

Virginia: When we had the comets striking Jupiter

a few years ago, what really happened?

Hathors: That was actually another rhythm, another level, the intergalactic level. The comet was coming from deep space. The comet's fragments broke into pieces and collided with Jupiter. At an energetic level, what occurred was that Jupiter received an acupuncture treatment which set off cascades of energy affecting you here on this planet. Not physical damage, just energetic effects. There was no real disturbance that science can determine which was caused by the comets' collision with Jupiter. But energetically there were many things that occurred as a result of that collision. On many subtle levels people were affected, including the emotional.

Virginia: So are we to understand that the complexities of all this make it very difficult for us to grasp while we are in a human body?

Hathors: Yes.

Virginia: Then what is your advice to us as we try to have some sense of stability and security while we're going through these things which we can't yet understand?

Hathors: Love more. Forgive more. And understand that love is not just a palliative; it's truly an energetic power that will lead you to the quickest and deepest space of stability. When you are able to enter into that vibrational state of love and acceptance, when you are able to forgive, then you are in a position that is *energetically unmovable*. Whatever happens around you will not be disturbing because you are in the Fundamental Tone, the fundamental octave that holds and binds the Universe together. Consequently, you are literally above it all and untouched by it. So it is our advice, in these times of disturbance, to love more and to forgive more. Start with loving and forgiving yourself to the best of your ability and extend it outward. We ask you to try the self-mastery exercises and to use our information about sound to assist yourself in this process.

Virginia: Could you just say a little bit more about

the sky goddess *Hator* and whether that concept is related in any way to the Sacred Elements?

Hathors: An indirect connection, yes. There was an understanding that the Source, the Mystery, expressed itself through the Four Elements, and air was the element most associated with the Divine. You need to understand that as the primitive consciousness looked at its reality, being Earth-bound, and dealing with three-dimensional reality, it seemed as if "the gods came from above," from the sky realm, so they would associate the Divine with the sky.

Hator, in her first manifestation, was the sky goddess. It was later that the Egyptians associated her with fertility. Thus the first goddess of the Egyptian pantheon (before the time of the Pharaohs) went through a metamorphosis in the minds of the people. At first she was associated with the element of air (the sky), and during this period she was seen as a manifestation of Divine love and ecstasy. Then she became associated with fertility and the Earth. It was also during this latter manifestation that she became associated with sex and joy. Love and ecstasy continued to be associated with her, as well. The work of the priestesses in the temples of *Hator* was double-natured. They were often asked to influence fertility and affect good births. This was the outer work of the temple. The esoteric (hidden) work of the temple was the use of alchemy, which involved the raising-up of the initiate's sexual energy to the higher energy centers of the body. The priestesses were well-versed in this esoteric science, and much of *tantra* can be traced back to these roots.

Now...we wish to leave you with these thoughts: Your body is the most sacred temple, for it is where heaven and Earth conjoin. Your life is a gift born from the Four Elements. Without them, the Universe would not exist. They respond to your love. Send them your gratitude and receive their message. Creation speaks to you through them with every breath you take, and with every beat of your heart. Be still and listen.

Chapter 9
The Fulcrum Point

We would now like to address what we see as one of the most opportune moments for your evolution and the acceleration of growth in human history. It has to do with the speeding up of events in this dimension so that, as we have said previously, you will be experiencing more and more awareness in less and less "clock" time. This is creating, and will continue to create, strong emotional reactions and feeling responses. The feelings and emotions that you are experiencing in this period of greater intensity are to be treasured, not avoided, for they are your modern-day initiations into higher consciousness. You do not need to enter a Mystery School these days for your various trainings and initiations, as once humans did in Egypt.

There, the ancient temples of Egypt were spread out along the Nile River in a successive order of difficulty and the initiates would go to these temples to receive instruction. Each temple would present them with some new situation to master. The temple initiations were part of their evolutionary process. Now, however, you do not need to go to Egypt or any other place to experience your initiations. The trials and tests that you face in your physical body, in your relationships, in your work, and in your spiritual endeavors are your modern day initiatory trials for higher consciousness. By viewing them in this way, the difficult experiences of your life can be experienced for what they are–initiations–instead of something to be avoided or something by which to feel victimized. Many humans call out "Why me?" and blame God for their negative circumstances because they do not understand the part their own consciousness plays in the unfolding of their lives.

We've called this chapter "The Fulcrum Point" because the metaphor of the fulcrum is an apt example in regard to understanding consciousness at the three-dimensional realm. The fulcrum is like the balance point of a childhood seesaw or teeter totter often seen in parks. Two children will sit at opposite ends of a narrow board that is supported in the center (the fulcrum); and the children take turns pushing up, forcing the other end of the seesaw (and child) to move down. The fulcrum point is the point at which the seesaw board pivots. As long as there is movement, there is the force of the polarities (up/down movement) on the fulcrum point. This is a beautiful metaphor for consciousness itself–for as consciousness moves into duality from its still-point of non-duality, opposite forces come into play. As with the seesaw, in your world of polarities, as something moves up, something else must move down and so on.

In your current life as a human being on this planet you are experiencing a rapid acceleration of many multi-dimensional forces–physical, mental, emotional, cultural, social, spiritual, global–and many of these are happening simultaneously. The fulcrum point for you, as a human being, is where these multi-dimensional forces interconnect in the present moment. If you've ever sat on a seesaw, you know that there is the possibility of a balance point in which the opposite ends of the seesaw are parallel to the ground and there is no movement. That moment is a perfect balancing of dualities, and the fulcrum point would be in a neutral state of friction or activity. However, when the dualities begin to move again (one end moves up while the other end moves down) the fulcrum point experiences an increase of activity and friction.

You, as a human being, experience that friction as an increase of pressure through the emotional or feeling nature–so that as events intensify, your feelings also intensify in the present moment. The point about which these feelings intensify is your fulcrum point. This is the *initiatory portal*. This is the doorway to your soul's accelerated evolution and ascended awareness. The fulcrum point of your life, moment to moment, instant to instant, is experienced within the most sacred temple of your physical body. How you deal with your experiences is your choice as an individual. Yet if you fail to see your life and this planet as a sacred space, fail to see this life as an initiatory process, then you may go into blame, discounting, or avoidance. There are many ways to avoid the present moment of one's life. However, if you align with this understanding that the events and experiences of your life are your initiatory process, then you will hold sacred whatever is occurring, even if it is difficult.

The initiatory process is essentially strewn with difficulties, tests and trials. For this is how the soul grows. Mastery over a particular level or domain of the self brings mastery to the soul. Fundamentally, you are working through the emotional, mental and spiritual "contents" of your own consciousness. And this is experienced through the events of your life, specifically the thoughts, feelings and emotions that these events trigger within you. If you honor the fulcrum point (the present moment of your life) as that center, that pivotal focus of your own consciousness, then you are prepared to move into a different relationship with your experience. Honor your experience and feeling responses, for they are the meaning, context and purpose of your life.

This very instant, you are using the experiences of your life, whatever they are, as footholds to climb the mountain of your own consciousness. From our understanding there is an element that needs to be added, and that is mastery of one's energy. You may have noticed that when your emotional reactions are strong or when things occur that are overwhelming, you are less able to deal effectively with them–less able to cope and make the right choices for yourself–and less able to use that opportunity as fuel for the transformation of your own consciousness. What we have often observed is that when people go into moments of intense overwhelm and slip into unconsciousness, they will attempt to avoid awareness of the present moment (the fulcrum point of their experience) by drifting, sleeping, overworking, or avoiding the whole thing in some other way such as drugs, food, or alcohol. For some of you, even meditation can be a subtle form of avoidance. The tools that we share in this material are meant to help you master your energy so that when you enter into a fulcrum or pivotal experience and the intensity of that moment increases, you have the energy mastery to align yourself positively.

You will have both the awareness of what is happening and the mastery of your energy fields to make correct choices for yourself in that moment. These two aspects together create a powerful vortex that allow you to flow quickly into higher levels of consciousness. Both must be in place, however. You must understand, appreciate and honor your life experience. Then you must use your feeling responses in the initiatory process to achieve the energy mastery that stabilizes and allows you to take advantage of these growth opportunities.

It is ironic and paradoxical that consciousness can create either a heaven or a hell around the same event. The reactions that you experience in response to various different events actually have very little to do with the events themselves. This is the initiatory awareness–the coming to understand that whatever occurs, you are creating your emotional or feeling responses, and you are responsible for them.

There are emotional states you tend to experience as hellish, a kind of purgatory, in which you are tormented by the demons of your own attachments—fears, pains, angers and sadnesses. And there are emotional states where you feel content, centered, loved and fulfilled. Simply recognize that these two polar states, heaven and hell, are within you, within your own consciousness, within your own being. They are not located physically in space anywhere. They are within you. They are polar opposites that work and move and pulsate from one to the other. The fulcrum point of your life experience is that edge on which they teeter. As you acquire this understanding and master your energy flows, you will be better able to balance the polarities within yourself.

Taking the metaphor of the fulcrum point even deeper, we would say that those events that seem to be happening externally are actually catalysts that create a response within you. The events themselves are essentially empty. They are triggers, however, that are causing something to respond from within your own consciousness. As you go through the initiatory process of your life you will have feelings or emotional responses to innumerable and often challenging things. This is your nature as a human. But if you experience these emotional feeling responses with awareness and self-compassion—look lovingly within yourself, so to speak—you will find the polarities within your own being that are creating your suffering. These polarities are ruled by your beliefs and choices from the deepest levels of your own consciousness.

The purpose and nature of initiation is to provide a mirror to reflect back to the soul so that it can clearly see and understand the choices it has made. The initiatory processes of your life that you are living today, and the people and the situations you encounter, are all holding a mirror for you. Consequently, when you experience something difficult, and if you do not look at what you are feeling inside of yourself in response to the event, you will miss a tremendous opening to greater awareness and clarity. This is the power of the fulcrum point. It is a sacred moment. Every moment of your experience is sacred and when you find yourself in situations that are difficult and challenging, know that you have entered another initiation opportunity. This makes it a time for rejoicing, a time for awareness, clarity and self-compassion. As you master the tools that we have given and will continue to give, your energy body will align in such a way that you will be able to take advantage of these initiatory experiences in a constructive and creative manner. So shall the soul advance.

We would now like to share a story, a legend, that we have in our culture concerning one human living in that earlier historical period you call ancient Egypt. In a way, this story symbolizes the current human experience on Earth.

It seems there was an initiate who came to the temple of *Hator* (*Hator*, the goddess of love and joy) desperately wanting to experience these states of love and joy. But he wanted to enter the initiation process at the highest level without going through the lower temples of the underworld. Each time the hopeful initiate would come to the *Hator* temple of love and joy, he would be sent away with the comment, "You are not ready. You must enter the underworld."

This person, being very crafty, used various disguises to present himself as a woman, a crippled man, a sage, or even a beggar. Yet he was still the same person and was sent away. Still he returned time and time again to the temple of *Hator*, wanting and seeking initiation into the mysteries, but without the willingness to go through the lower temples first. Every time he appeared in disguise, he was sent back to the underworld where he refused to enter and begin the initiation process which would have eventually earned him his heart's desire. The point of this tale is that *you cannot bypass your own underworld. You must go down into the catacombs of your own unconsciousness before seeking the higher spiritual mysteries.*

You see, the higher you go in consciousness the deeper you must delve to remain in balance. If you go too high in consciousness without balancing your hidden depths, including your own unconsciousness, then you are unbalanced and potentially dangerous. Why? Because then you are acting without awareness of the crucial parts of yourself that are in your own underworld–those aspects that are not evolved, such as your angers, your hatreds, your jealousies, your rages, your fantasies, even your death wishes. These things that you try to keep out of awareness are part of your human nature and *your task as a human being is to integrate and to heal all levels of your experience in this dimension!*

One of those levels of this experience which must be healed has to do with what you call darkness, which we call unawareness. The darkness is unawareness. The task of evolution, as we see it, is to expand awareness so that it is all-encompassing and becomes incorporated into all of your beingness. The processes, the circumstances, and events that are occurring on your planet at this time are of such an intense nature that they are activators for those feelings and beliefs that live in your underworld. The fulcrum point of experience, the intensity of the moment-by-moment experiences of life, are the initiatory portals allowing you to move into an awareness and understanding of the depths of yourself. Never doubt your nature is profoundly capable of this task for your consciousness includes the light, the celestial realms of your own being, as well as the dark demonic worlds of your own being. To hold these two polarities in compassion, consciousness, and love is to balance them and to heal the darkness through the power and the light of awareness. This is the task of evolution, as we see it, for this level and your dimension. Your Earth is evolving, arising into a higher level of awareness, vibration, and consciousness and so, friends of Earth, are you.

Now Virginia, do you have questions for us?

Virginia: Greetings again. My first question today, suggested by information in this chapter, but in other places as well, concerns your advice regarding what humans presently term "psychology." Could you comment about our present effectiveness in using psychology for healing purposes? Also what do you recommend that our counselors and psychologists do in order to understand and apply energy as a part of their personal and professional process?

Hathors: Psychology as practiced currently on Earth is extremely limited. Its outcomes are very limited and the understanding of most psychologists is very narrow from our understanding and perspective. Psychology, for the most part, aims at getting humans to adjust to their society in a way that creates as little difficulty for the individuals as possible. So the basic vision or goal is simply one of adaptation. And this adaptation is to a society that is essentially oppressive in regard to human potential. The human being has far greater potential for expression and emotional and mental experience than is conceived of by most psychologies. Many psychologies deal with areas of consciousness that are language based, which requires much talking, and very little time is focused on resolving fundamental *energy* issues.

You see, everything that is held emotionally in the body and in the subtle fields as a distortion, as pain, or as trauma, has an energetic component. Therefore, one can talk and talk but nothing will fundamentally have changed because the energetics have not been addressed. So we would say that if individuals working in this field wish to expand themselves and their repertoire to become more effective in healing work, they should include the energetics of emotion and mental states in their methodology—so that the emotions and the energetics of those emotions are addressed directly with their clients.

When the energetics of a situation are addressed, then the trauma, the discomfort, is resolved and the nervous system and behavior come back into a state of equilibrium and balance. This brings an increase of wellness in the individual. And from that stable platform, one can then reach the higher mystical, spiritual states of consciousness that heighten effectiveness as ascending human beings. Without addressing the emotional state, and their energetic components, you simply avoid the problem.

Even worse is the use of drugs to suppress the energies. Because it is possible to chemically alter the brain so that emotional problems can actually be suppressed, a person becomes dependent on the drug to achieve a semi-state, a quasi-state of chemically-induced balance. However, as soon as the drug is withdrawn, the person comes back into chaos because the original energies persist, so this is not a solution. This is just making matters worse. There is a relationship between brain chemistry and the energetics of emotion and thought forms and beliefs, but the science of it on Earth is in its infancy. The methods you now use to control brain chemistry with drugs are like using a club to hit a gnat. One needs to be more subtle, more gentle and more discreet.

Virginia: Thank you. Could you comment on earlier practices of shock treatment using electricity and other devices?

Hathors: It is simply devastating to the person's field, to the nervous system, and it creates rips and tears in their subtle bodies. Since the etheric body is damaged, especially the *Ka*, or *pranic* body, shock treatment is a very, very poor choice. There are some occasions where it is effective in creating a behavior change in terms of suppressing certain emotions when everything else has failed. But it's not really understood in the psychology of your day as to why shock treatments sometimes work. It has been observed that it sometimes does help. However, it often leaves the person without memory and with other problems in their energetic fields that are not observed because the observers are not sensitive enough to sense what happened to the auric field. The reason that a shock treatment works at all is because when there is a bolus or a surge of energy into the brain and its biochemicals, it's as if an explosion has gone off and the brain comes back to a different type of equilibrium than it had before. Sometimes that equilibrium is better and sometimes it is worse, but it is a very poor, clumsy, crude method to alter brain chemistry and activity.

Virginia: Thank you. Then do you perceive any use of electromagnetic energies in doing emotional healing?

Hathors: Yes, and this will become clearer during the coming decades. Sound will also be used much more in the treatment of emotional and mental problems as well as electromagnetics, and of course the use of magnets will become much more understood in this regard.

Virginia: You've spoken about wellness. How is it that poor health in the physical body affects or influences our attempt to balance these two inner polarities that you speak about here in "The Fulcrum Point" chapter?

Hathors: If the vitality of the *Ka* is not strong enough, then one cannot balance energy polarities nor can one take full advantage of the initiatory opportunities in one's life. If one is fatigued and exhausted, one simply cannot focus; it's not possible. One has to go to sleep or rest and recoup one's energy before one can focus again.

Virginia: So if there is a chronic degenerative condition, as many people on the planet are experiencing, especially those in technological countries, what advice or recommendations do you have for us in order to do the best we can to balance these inner polarities?

Hathors: This is a wide topic and in practice things would be tailored to the individual rather than giving broad sweeping information. However, we'll employ a broad sweep in an attempt to answer your question. As we said earlier, the vitality of the planet is decreasing as a result of the loss of minerals and the decrease of oxygen. So, basically, what you can do at a biological level is to increase the levels of minerals and oxygen. This increase will help many, many conditions that are now being experienced. Recently your scientists have uncovered something called colloidal minerals which will be found to be very helpful in this regard.

There are also products and substances that increase the oxygenation of your bodies. Eating more live foods will help the entire process, specifically sprouts and young, tender greens before they become mature. These hold within themselves a very high level of complex proteins and minerals that will help in this process. So eating more live foods with the enzymes undamaged will assist this process of mineralization and increase the absorption of oxygen. This requires your soil to be healthy and pure, of course; and the same for water.

At the physical level these are a few things that will help greatly. But it's a synergetic process of doing everything you can to increase your vitality, including clarification and elevation of your beliefs and interactions with others. As you strengthen the *Ka*, the life-force, then other aspects of your consciousness will be strengthened. You will have more focus; you will have more energy and stamina.

At the emotional level there is another aspect to consider. Remember that the thought forms and the emotional movements of energy taking place in the planetary mass consciousness tend to degrade life-force, tend to pull life-force out. So as you become a sensitive life-force person, you must protect your energy. Your life energy is precious and you don't give it away to just anybody. You keep it for your own enhancement and those who are close to you. So you don't give energy away frivolously and you don't take on the negative emotional patterns or the emotional neediness of others. Why? This is one of the things that drains life-force quicker than anything. In our experience of Earth we often observe the misuse of emotion and the misuse of emotional need.

As we previously mentioned, this planet is a school for emotion so it is a very intensely emotional place where emotions abound. And this will only increase as the planet, and this entire area of the solar system, increases in vibratory rate. So those who give their own energy away "to take care of others" will find their energy depleted. This depletion of your energy comes directly out of your *Ka*. As you become more sensitive to energy in general and to your own energy in particular, you can sense when someone is drawing your energy out, or when you're giving it away. You will feel fatigued and drained.

Virginia: So is that a warning to all of us?

Hathors: Definitely. It's a particular warning to all humans who are *emotional caretakers*. One can so completely take care of another person emotionally that one has nothing left for oneself and this is not spiritual enlightenment or attainment. This is simply misuse of energy. It may come out of a place of compassion, of wanting to help the other person, but if you have drained yourself in the process then you have damaged yourself, your *Ka*, your own vitality, and this is not good.

Virginia: Agreed. And we do appreciate this message. Now, regarding your explanation of the fulcrum point, it's been my experience that many young people today have never been on a seesaw in the park. So I'm asking if there's another analogy you can use to clarify the fulcrum point?

Hathors: We would say to those who haven't yet experienced a seesaw to, by all means, go and experience one! However, we can offer a computer analogy. The joystick is a device that many people use while playing computer games. If you have used a computer game you will know exactly what we mean. When the joystick is pulled to the left, the little image or the character on the screen will do something, and when it's pulled far to the right it will do the opposite. So you have two polarities–to the left is one action, to the right is another action–and so the same principle applies. You can swing back and forth between left and right and have two opposing actions.

Virginia: Yes. Thank you for that. Has there ever been a civilization or a culture here on Earth that actually achieved a balanced fulcrum point?

Hathors: Yes, there has been. However, one needs to understand that when we're dealing with civilizations we're dealing with individuals, and within a civilization's population stream you may have 100,000 who have attained a fulcrum point position and another 3,000,000 who have not. But a general principle would be that if no one in a given culture has attained a balanced fulcrum point then the entire culture, by definition, would be in chaos. So it needs to be understood that the fulcrum point is something that is attained by individuals, not by the civilization. It's only when you have amassed enough individuals who have attained balance within a cultural stream that the civilization gains a balanced fulcrum point. There was a general sense of stability in the Golden Age of Egypt, the Golden Age of Greece, Lemuria, and even Atlantis had a certain level of attainment and balance before they overemphasized the mental.

Virginia: In Egypt, was that in the time of *Thoth*?

Hathors: Yes, in the time of *Thoth*.

Virginia: So does this imply that the *Hathor* civilization, which you say has ascended, didn't all happen simultaneously? Or let me just ask how you explain your present ascended civilization in terms of reaching some kind of a fulcrum point somewhere along the way?

Hathors: That is a most intriguing question that no one has ever asked before, although it seems quite obvious. We would not say that we entered the state of ascension simultaneously but it was very close. At the moment that we entered this dimension through the portal of Sirius, we were already an ascended civilization. We came here as ascended beings. The reason we were requested to come to assist *this* ascension process was because we reached ascension on our planet in a similar fashion, though not exactly like what is occurring on Earth. So there was a very strong resonance because we had gone through something similar.

Virginia: ...in your own Universe?

Hathors: Yes, as mentioned this was beyond Sirius which is a portal to this dimension. We were actually in another dimension, another Universe prior to coming here.

Virginia: So because of the experience you had by mastering your own emotional nature–that's what achieved your ascension, your accreditation?

Hathors: Yes. Yes, our credentials. We are considered masters of love and sound and the reason we are masters of love is because we have balanced the emotional body and we have anchored ourselves in the Great Mystery. It is the potential for all humans to be anchored and balanced in love, for love is the highest coherent emotion generated by humans. It is a powerful focal point and balance point within the human emotional body. What is going on now is that there are a multitude of emotions playing out as a result of several billion peoples' different thought forms, beliefs, and perceptions. This creates all types of emotional responses.

Nonetheless, in terms of human evolution, love is where you are heading–it is your potential to experience the emotion of love continuously on all levels of consciousness. This is something that we have attained and that is why we are aligned with you; and this is why many beings from other realms throughout the Universe are observing you. They can observe your situation and your emotional responses even though some of the beings observing you don't have feelings and emotions themselves. They yearn to have it. It's a missing piece for them and the funny thing is that many humans avoid what these beings find desirable, namely feelings and emotions.

Virginia: Do you have an explanation of why the

Earth is a training school for learning the emotion of love?

Hathors: Well, it goes back to the beginnings and it has to do with the unfolding of Earth and its position in relationship to the physical Sun. Here on Earth the development of vegetation and the oxygen stream that surrounds it enabled life, as you know it, to emerge. And there is a vital relationship between emotion and oxygen as your methods of working with the breath that the yogis call *pranayama* demonstrate. Altering the breath to balance emotion is founded in this understanding that oxygen and life-force, or *prana*, hold a direct relationship to emotion. So you have a planet which has developed an environment that is highly conducive to experiencing emotion which was recognized quite early by many cultures and civilizations intergalactically. Thus, the word went out and souls deliberately incarnated to experience this opportunity.

Virginia: That's very interesting. I felt you'd give us further clarity. Now do you think of anything else you would like to add?

Hathors: In terms of the fulcrum point, no.

Virginia: Then we give you our thanks.

THE HATHOR MATERIAL

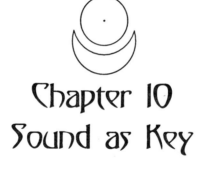

Chapter 10
Sound as Key

All things in the manifest Universe are vibrational in nature. Your science continues to uncover this truth that everything that exists is vibrational, that all things have sound or vibration as well as form, and that the forms and vibrations are interchangeable. There is a direct relationship between the form of something and its frequency of vibration. From our perspective you are complex interconnecting fields of energy, including light and sound. The various cells that comprise the organs and systems of your body emit sound vibrations (frequencies) that are complex and interconnect with other cells, thus causing cellular resonances. In fact, *the entire universe of your body is a walking symphony.* This is not a metaphor, for you are luminous eggs of cascading energy, creating multiple cascading resonances of sound. Your body, for instance, is a standing wave pattern created through many forces, and these various standing waves that comprise your body are in resonance to the Earth–and are also affected by the resonant shifts that the Earth is going through.

At present, the Earth is going through a major transitory period in which its own resonances and vibrations are altering and moving to a new state of balance. Therefore, the resonance fields of your body are also transiting to a new level of balance from the subatomic, atomic, on up to the cellular, and are affecting your organs and systems. This is creating tremendous internal biological stresses which get translated into physical challenges that sometimes take the form of diseases and sometimes the form of fatigue or agitated states. In the emotional realm it takes the form of emotional instability.

Emotions also have sound and vibration for they are actually a multilevel phenomenon which include neurological patterns within the brain. The hormonal responses within your body also relate to the changes in emotion. Emotion affects changes in breathing patterns and oxygenation in the blood, as well as changes in blood chemistry. All of these changes set off specific harmonics. These vibrational changes can be detected and your science is on the verge of doing so. You will soon find that all emotions have a sound or vibratory signature. Thus all emotions will come to be viewed much like musical chords, some of which are melodic and soothing while others are grating and cacophonous.

It is also true that sound or the signature of emotion is held intercellularly through resonant fields in specific areas of your body. What we mean by this is that an emotion such as anger and its sound signature, will have a certain quality to it–a certain timbre, a certain pitch, a certain intensity. That sound signature will emerge from the cells, the cellular resonances of your body, in a *specific area*. Many people feel their anger in the upper chest area and in the peripheral areas of the arms. Sadness is often experienced within the heart area and also within and around the eyes. *So every emotion or emotional reaction has a place of origin within the intercellular resonant fields of the body.* And these emotional reactions or patterns have specific effects in terms of the chemistry and electromagnetic field patterns of the body.

The suppression of emotion is not a healthy thing. The "stuffing" of emotion, to use one of your terms, actually causes a backlash within the biochemistry of the body. Since we see you primarily as energy bodies, or luminous eggs, emitting cascading resonances of sound and vibration, we notice that when you purposely suppress emotion, the sound signature moves deeper into the cellular structure of the body. If you have enough resonances repeatedly moving down and being suppressed over and over again so that the emotion or energy is held deep within the cells, you can actually begin to create a negative physical effect. Your physical body will create symptoms of those unexperienced emotions. For instance, rage can be translated into physical symptoms of high blood pressure; and there are many other examples of how emotion can be translated into physical symptoms as a result of successive suppression of emotional energy.

In our discussion of this vital topic, we will explain three areas or levels having to do with sound or vibration. The first one which we've begun to explore has to do with emotion, the signature of emotion, and *the expression of emotion through sound as a beneficial phenomena*, a beneficial technique, if you will. The second area has to do with *the use of sound to activate specific states of consciousness*, and thirdly we wish to describe *the use of sound or vibration as a way to deliberately affect physical processes within the body.*

To more clearly understand emotion, we recommend that you view yourself as a complex resonant field of energy and vibration, acknowledging that emotions have sound signatures which you can express vocally as a sigh, a yell, a scream, a laugh, or even just a noise. Then you can allow your awareness to encompass the areas of your body where the emotions are being held so that facilitating their release is possible. We will propose a series of experiments, if you are unfamiliar with this process, so that you may become attuned to the truth and the method by which you can allow emotion to express and clear itself through sound. To prepare for the next exercise, recall an emotion that you experience on a regular basis, be it anger, sadness, or joy.

༳༳༳༳ **SELF-MASTERY EXERCISE # 5** ༳༳༳༳

Simply allow yourself to recall one particular emotion and its feeling response. Then relax as you feel or recall the emotion, letting your awareness surround the vast intercellular universe of your physical body from head to toe. Now focus and sense where within your body this emotion is experienced. It may be subtle but there will be a resonant vibration somewhere in your body in response to the emotion. Allow your awareness to move into this area of your body where the emotion resides and then take a deep breath, allowing yourself to make the sound of the emotion as you exhale.

This is not a rational thought process. This is a totally spontaneous, intuitive, biological, physical process. This is something you do naturally, but this natural process has become difficult for some people because of the ways they have been educated and raised.

Children let themselves spontaneously express what they are feeling through crying, laughing, yelling, or some other sound until they have been told that they cannot do this and must be quiet. But the natural biological impulse is to make a sound in response to an especially strong emotion. So, for some of you adults, retraining yourself to do what the human system does naturally–what you did as a child before you were conditioned to be still–is very important. Now we are not suggesting a return to babyhood or childishness that is disruptive or chaotic; but we are suggesting that you re-own this aspect of your natural biological inheritance.

There are things to be said for keeping social peace; however, when it is taken too far, the body will pay a price for suppressing emotional energy instead of allowing an outward expression to occur. Emotional energy can be cleared through the vocal cords, through bodily movement, or both, instead of getting pushed down into the intercellular resonant fields to create a type of unhealthy cellular tension. Stress begins because the cellular fields must hold this suppressed emotion both as sound or vibration and induce other biological factors, such as the chemical changes that take place when one suppresses emotion. The process of preventing or releasing stress is quite simple once you become aware of it, and you can use this method to quickly clear negative emotions that arise day by day, so your energy body remains healthy.

For example, as we said, when you experience something that creates an emotional response in you, you can deliberately move your awareness to the area of your body where you feel that emotional response instead of ignoring or denying it. You can even allow yourself to get in touch with the sound that naturally wants to express itself and then dare to make that sound. Yes, allow the sound to emerge from the emotion. It may be laughing, grunting or groaning, crying; it may be yelling, or even screaming. It may be notes such as in a musical scale, toning, or some such sound. Whatever it is, you allow it to express itself in its original innocence without forcing it to be anything in particular. This will actually clear emotional energy from your field.

We recommend that you use this sound technique on a regular basis in order to clear up emotional energy and to achieve balance. You might begin making these sound expressions in private places where no one will hear or disturb you. But you can also make these sounds very softly at any convenient time. The most important thing is to encourage yourself to become aware of any emotion that you are experiencing and allow its sound signature to emerge from that emotion through your voice. Keep making the sound until you feel relieved and clear. That is the technique. It is very simple and it works.

The second level of this material we wish to discuss concerns sound as a means to activate or access specific states of consciousness. From an energetic standpoint, every state of consciousness has its own energetic signature, including vibratory signatures within the various subtle bodies and their relationships to each other. Then as one moves through different states of awareness–be it waking, sleeping, or the so-called super states of consciousness (i.e., spiritual states like *samadhi* and other states of meditation)–there are specific sound signatures or vibratory signatures, as well. It is possible to use sound to access these different states of consciousness. This is an ancient science that can be traced back through many different traditions on your planet which have used precise sounds (sometimes termed *mantras*) as keys to unlock specific levels of awareness and consciousness.

Because sound is an ancient science from so many different cultural traditions and time periods, it is not in the scope of our discussion to build upon these or comment upon their very vast and complex nature. However, we can give some simple suggestions on using sound to access different states of consciousness, since it is similar to what is used for clearing emotion.

ॐॐॐॐ **SELF-MASTERY EXERCISE # 6** ॐॐॐॐ

Allow yourself to pause now and feel a deep sense of peace (...pause...). Simply permit yourself to make any sound at all that best represents the feeling of peace to you.

What sound came forth? Now repeat that sound and remember it for future use. Under stress you can simply make this same peaceful sound and shift your focus back to peace again. Anytime in your daily life you experience any useful states of awareness that you find particularly helpful, merely allow your awareness to move into a sense of that state of consciousness, especially the feeling of that state, and permit a sound or series of sounds to emerge from that state. Listen to the sounds that you make. The sounds that you make from this state of awareness will be a reflection of the sound signature itself. This will allow you to access that state again, any time you desire.

There are two elements, then, that will allow you to access specific states of awareness, and these are a combination of the *feeling* of it and the *sound signature* of it. If you were to meditate and reach a deep state of profound peace and calm, in that moment you could intend awareness to encompass that feeling and then allow a sound or series of sounds to emerge through your voice. Listening to the sound you make while being aware of the feeling provides a strong means of anchoring these experiences so that you can bring them back at any future time. The two together are extremely powerful because all feelings also have sound signatures and you are just bringing two elements of one essential, fundamental relationship into conscious awareness.

It is wonderfully empowering to bring any specific, positive state that you have experienced in the past back into the present moment. So if during the original experience you can allow an awareness of the feeling response within yourself, along with the sound signature of that state, then you can bring back that state of consciousness simply by feeling it and making the sounds. This is a very easy technique and, like the first one, it works extraordinarily well. What this activity requires, however, is an appreciation of, and a mastery of, yourself as a complex field of resonances and vibrations that express themselves as feelings, emotions, and sound. Identifying and expressing the appropriate combination for the effect you desire, or outcome you wish to explore and to experience, is a step up in expanded consciousness.

The third way sound can be a valuable consciousness key has to do with the ability of sound or vibration to affect physical processes, especially physical processes within the body, for healing. *It is* possible to affect physical processes within your own body or the body of another person through the sounds that you make in response to the intention that you hold in consciousness.

Sound vibration can actually affect the resonant fields within intercellular processes down into the genetic levels, even down into the atomic and subatomic levels. The key is the right use of intention, awareness, and sound. This is the triad that will allow you to begin to actually affect physical matter through the agency of consciousness expressing itself through sound. This is a vast domain and there is no room to fully discuss it in the short space that we have here. However, it is possible to begin to work in this area with what we have already given you. As you explore this area new insights will come to you.

Fundamentally, it is important to remember that all matter, regardless of what form it takes, is essentially vibrational in nature. Therefore, by using the right vibrations it is possible to cause that particular form to resonate or vibrate in response. Using awareness, using intention and using the sound of your own voice, it is possible to affect any level of manifest creation. This is one of your birthrights, yet mastery of this does not occur until you have expanded your awareness enough to create such strong, clear intentions that the sounds you allow to emerge are precise enough. When these vibrations come together you have a powerful force that can literally change physical states at any level, unbelievable as this may seem to some people. It is our wish to encourage all humans to understand and incorporate these basic qualities of sound usage and healing into their everyday lives.

Now, Virginia, do you have questions?

Virginia: We have many people who tell us that they don't have the ability to sense where an emotion is being held inside of their body. Therefore to ask them to make a sound to express an emotion they can't locate is very challenging. What remarks and advice do you have for them?

Hathors: Those individuals would benefit from

becoming aware of physical sensation. All that is happening here is that consciousness, which can be aware of something in detail, can also be completely unaware of something that is occurring. For instance, you may be breathing right now but you are not necessarily aware of it. So things do happen in the body without awareness. If you are unable to experience the subtle sensations of emotion, then simply begin to train your consciousness to deliberately become aware of the body so that the sensations do become apparent. Here are several things we suggest.

One would be for the person to take a deep breath, then exhale and then hold the breath out. Direct your conscious awareness in the lungs and feel the buildup of sensation as the lungs yearn to take the next breath. There will be a tension in the lungs and a tension in the general thoracic area of the body. This tension will build and build until the lungs finally take the needed first breath. We would suggest holding off on taking that breath until you really can't hold the breath any longer. Then take that breath and feel the breath coming into the lungs. Feel the relief that the lungs and the thoracic area feel as the breath comes in. Do this several times. Do this as a regular little practice, if you will, to become aware of tension because the polarity of sensation in the body is expressed as tension or relaxation at different levels. So an emotion in the body will be felt as tension or relaxation. There will be other qualities as well, and as a person becomes aware of subtle physical sensation, the location of the emotion in the body will reveal itself.

Virginia: What recommendations do you have for those people who are very embarrassed or fearful of allowing themselves to make unique sounds–particularly if they think they aren't musical or have no talent?

Hathors: People need to understand that releasing or making sounds has nothing to do with musical ability, a beautiful voice, or any of that. It's the organized expression of energy through the voice that has many benefits. Using the vocal center, at the throat *chakra*, to express and balance energy has tremendous benefits far outweighing the embarrassment. If people feel like they are not able to make sound around others, then we suggest they go off somewhere alone. Many people are by themselves in their cars when they drive and this is a great place to make sounds—or in a room where no one else is around. But we would say they should practice until they become comfortable with the sound of their own voice.

Embarrassment about making sounds is fundamentally an emotional issue—an energetic block—because the flow of creative energy as it moves up into the throat center wants to be expressed through word and the power to create through the word. If one is holding back, out of embarrassment, from making sound, it is probably due to an earlier emotional experience of being "squashed," repressed or made wrong for expressing oneself. It may be a whole pattern of holding back one's truth, one's energy. This type of emotional block needs to be resolved, because if one is unwilling to make sound using one's vocal chords, then one is choosing to constrain one's energy.

Virginia: Is this related to stuttering?

Hathors: Yes, there is a relationship...a direct relationship.

Virginia: So it's again the same suppression or holding back?

Hathors: Yes.

Virginia: I understand that when stutterers participate in a chorus, or pretend to be someone else, they don't stutter.

Hathors: Right. It's an emotional block that's held within language patterns of the brain. When language patterns engage and the person has to express them, then an emotional trigger goes off. Because the deeper parts of the brain are not able to handle the signal, the person stutters. It is fundamentally an emotional block. When the emotion is resolved then the nervous system and the brain come back into balance and stuttering will not be a problem.

Virginia: Then there may be hope in the future for some stutterers?

Hathors: We would say from the deeper levels of our understanding that most humans are stutterers. Not that you stutter out loud where people can hear, but that you hold back your truth and don't state it clearly. That, to us, is a type of stuttering and that is an emotional block.

Virginia: Interesting. Now there is a term used in this chapter that I really want to clarify. Can you be very precise about the meaning of "sound signature?"

Hathors: Yes. A sound signature is the same as a signature on paper. For example, when you sign a check at your bank, if the signature is identical to the original signature on file, it's a match and the account opens up magically. Even if you have the proper identification, however, if the signature does not match, the bank personnel won't open the account and you can't withdraw anything. The same with sound signatures. All emotion, all thought forms, beliefs, and energies have a sound pattern that may contain one or more frequencies of vibration. When these vibrations or sound patterns are expressed by an individual–or sometimes mechanically–so that the sound signature matches the fundamental signature, you get a resonance. Then that emotion or thought form emerges into consciousness.

To be precise about this, the emotion of sadness, for instance, has a sound signature that most humans would recognize as crying. The act of crying, the sound of weeping, is recognized universally as the sound signature for sadness, grief, or loss when that emotion is expressing itself as a sound pattern. But, if someone suppresses their sadness instead of experiencing it in the moment, the sound or the vibration energetically coils up inside the field, waiting in dormancy for an opportunity to express itself. At the first opportunity, the sadness suddenly un-coils, spirals out, and one finds oneself crying. You can know this is true if you find yourself crying at relatively inappropriate times, like watching television programs or certain movies that touch your feelings. In these moments, you know the depth of feeling is far vaster than what is appropriate for the event you are watching. All that is happening is that your viewing has set off a resonance, the current signature has matched the fundamental sig-nature, and now it is uncoiling, "un-spiraling," and expressing itself. Similarly, all suppressed emotions will coil up energetically in the field and uncoil when ex-pressed.

As the energies on your planet increase, more emo-tions will be triggered in yourself and others; and often you will not know where they come from or what has trig-gered them. Often times you may not know what to do with them! Our suggestion is, if an emotion arises, find an appropriate space, make the sound of the emotion and let it move through you. If you feel like crying, cry, so that you have cleared the energy, cleared that center, cleared the field of that suppressed emotion. This allows you to be more energetically balanced than before. As emotion arises, know that there is a sound within it. If you can make the sound and let yourself feel whatever it is–even if you don't know what it is–you will have assisted your-self in clearing. In that process, most of the time, you will begin to have an understanding of what the emotion is about.

Virginia: Let me see. Is there such a thing as a com-bined sound signature, or just a single one? Or are we talking here of a multiplicity that each of us expresses in our own way?

Hathors: Each of us expresses. We express our emo-tions through an emotional sound signature, as well. All beings, whether human or otherwise, must express any emotion in terms of sound or vibration.

Virginia: Are we identified by our sound signature as a composite? I'm not sure that I'm asking the right question.

Hathors: Well, yes. Let us put it this way. If you were to meet two people at the same time but did not know who they were–and one was an ascended master and one was a murderer–without knowing anything about these two you would feel something very different from each of them. This energy frequency is held within the emotional sound signatures within each of their fields. The ascended master will have balanced all the emotions so that the sound signature would be one of complete peace and utter calm. The other person would have such agitation as a result of these negative emotions and conflicting emotional sound signatures, that there would be a state of agitation.

Virginia: So it's the composite or the total of all of those emotions working together that identifies who we are. Was that ever used in any Mystery Schools?

Hathors: Oh, yes.

Virginia: Could you make a quick comment?

Hathors: When the initiates would come in to be reviewed before the next initiatory phase or ritual, they would be scanned by the priests and priestesses in just this manner. They would be scanned for their sound signatures, their emotional balance, to sense where they were balanced and where they were unbalanced. If they were balanced enough, the initiates would be allowed to proceed to the next level. If they were not balanced enough, they would be sent back to work on themselves because to go into an initiatory phase without balance would be dangerous.

Virginia: Does humanity now, through the removal of negative emotions, acquire a higher sound signature that allows advancement into higher realms?

Hathors: Absolutely, yes. We would say that while the spirit of what you said is true, to be precisely accurate, one does not remove negative emotions, one transmutes them.

Virginia: Thank you. Please say more.

Hathors: It's a belief of many humans that negative emotions and negative experiences need to be plucked out, and that's not truly accurate because they are an expression of the individual's fundamental perception of reality. What actually has to occur is that the emotion is transmuted and the system comes into balance and there is nothing to pluck out. The energy that has been congested is now free and contributing to the evolution of the individual instead of holding the person back. Energy must always be dealt with. One does not simply remove it.

Virginia: In terms of sound signatures, how does that relate to resonances of sound and shifts of resonances?

Hathors: How are you using the term "resonances" here?

Virginia: Earlier you indicated that the resonance fields are transiting through a level that created tremendous biological stresses. And that we need to understand the resonances of sound. You talk about the multiple cascading resonances of sound when you see us as a luminous egg...

Hathors: In this context, the resonances are between the organs of the body. Each organ of the body—well, let's take it subtler—each cell of the body has a resonant field. Even the atoms, the molecular structures that make up the cells, have their own resonance. But when you get to the level of the cells you start to have very complex overtones and resonances, and when you collect millions and millions of cells together to create tissues and organs, you have very complex sound matrices indeed.

A resonance is, for example, the heart in relationship to the kidneys. That fundamental resonance establishes a balance between the connection of these organs—and we're speaking of an energetic connection, not a functional connection, because medical science would say these are two very different functions. However, from an energetic standpoint, the heart emerges out of the kidney function. The Chinese are very clear in their understanding of this. So when the kidneys are strong, the heart can be strong. When the kidneys are weak, often the heart is weak. A healthy body's fundamental resonance establishes a balance, and so each of the organs has a resonant field of energy that is in a relationship, harmonically if you will, to all the other organs. To be in health is literally to be in harmony. Thus the resonances, the sounds and frequencies that are emitted by all the different organs must be in harmonic relationship to obtain and maintain health. Disease occurs when something goes out of harmonic relationship.

What is happening on the planet right now is a tremendous challenge to all biological systems because, as the planetary vibratory rate increases, everything is increasing in its vibratory rate clear down to the atomic, molecular level. So the cells and tissues that make up the organs are also being agitated, as it were, and because of emotional issues some organs will transit up faster than others.

For instance, just as a general viewpoint, the liver often holds suppressed anger. The kidneys often hold suppressed fear. The lungs often hold suppressed grief, and there are other organ/emotions as well. As the entire system is starting to go up in vibratory rate, the unexpressed emotions held in different organs will keep these organs at a lower level of vibration while the rest of the system is going upwards. When you have a vibratory imbalance between different organs, you have the beginning of disharmony between the harmonic resonances of the body. There is another reason why people are experiencing an explosion of emotions that are very strong, run very deep, and are very rapid. This is because the organs that are holding the emotions are literally discharging them in order to catch up with this vibratory shift.

Virginia: So the resonance shifts that the Earth goes through puts this additional stress on us humans?

Hathors: Yes.

Virginia: Thank you very much. Could you comment on how sound has been misused by previous Earth civilizations? We've understood that misuse may have happened in Atlantis, for one. Do you have any clarification about this you could share?

Hathors: Sound has been misused in many civilizations, but when it was brought to a high level or high degree of sophistication it was very destructive indeed! Atlantis was working with free energy and sound was a crucial part of this. Because they got so mental in their perspective and they disconnected from their own biological roots–once again we come back to this–they became very unbalanced and they destroyed themselves.

There was a misuse of sound again in Egypt that took place in the Pharaonic period, as you make the transition from Heliopolis to the Memphite era. This misuse was done by the priesthood, and that was part of the contribution to the decline of Egypt.

In many cultures, sound is misused and it is becoming a tool of warfare. Though not generally known among the populace, sound is now a weapon of war. So unless your global civilization gets back to its senses in honoring the Earth and all life, your civilization could create something similar to what happened in Atlantis.

Virginia: Another question about the emotional body. I was told one time by the being known as Christ Jesus that we constantly lose our love at the emotional level which causes this continuing anguish that our spiritual teachers are attempting to have us heal. Do you have any additional comments or examples of what we might do to get through this barrier of emotional limitation and anguish at the functional level?

Hathors: This is another very complex question, and it is a very profound question that was both asked and resolved in Egypt by a system known as Alchemy. In order to reduce something extremely complex down to its simplest terms, we would say that your emotional response to any given situation is a result of your perception of that situation. If you are sensing and experiencing a situation through the eyes of duality–which was expressed in the alchemical system of Egypt as the serpent of *Apophis*, the serpent of duality–then you get caught up in the battle of the senses of this third-dimensional reality. Here you interpret the event as being good or bad, positive or negative, as related to yourself. If it is good you may be elated; if you interpret it as bad, then you go into depression or anger or whatever your familiar pattern is.

If you experience a situation through what is called the left eye of *Horus*, through the intuitive faculty–or through the eye of *Thoth*, which is known as the eye of wisdom, the function of which is called *"tehuti"*–then you sense something beyond the physical. Since whatever is occurring in the physical realm is illusory in nature, your freedom comes when you see the truth behind the illusion. One still experiences the physical reality, but at an emotional level one senses something beyond the physical through the intuitive eye of *Horus* or through the eye of *Thoth*, the wisdom faculty. Indeed, this ability to sense the truth behind the illusion is known, in the Egyptian alchemical system, as *"maat."*

This truth behind the illusion is the ground from which all things emerge and it is essentially ever peaceful and calm, ever unchanging, compassionate, benevolent, and loving in nature. So *maat* is the fundamental aspect that holds everything. When one uses one's function of intuitive alignment with the higher aspects, and cultivates and perceives everything that happens in life through the intuitive function, one becomes grounded in the essential love and balance of all things. Then one is not thrown off course by the serpent of *Apophis*, the serpent of duality.

Virginia: So again it's giving up judgment, the good and the bad?

Hathors: Yes, good and bad are concepts created by the intellect. Life, in its infinite complexity, is not "black or white."

Virginia: So–as our religions advise–judgment is one of the stumbling blocks we keep coming up against?

Hathors: Yes, we want to be very precise here. We are not saying to give up the intellect. The intellect is very crucial in the evolution of consciousness! We are saying do not be seduced by the conditioning of the intellect to accept what appears to be reality. For in the understanding of higher dimensions, what is happening in a lower dimension is only a piece of the puzzle. There is something far vaster and greater that is creating effects. So be in touch with that Source behind everything!

Virginia: Now I wonder what you have noticed that we humans are doing successfully from an energetic standpoint–among those of us who are at least attempting the awakening process–to activate or access states of higher consciousness? And what else can we do to accelerate our process?

Hathors: From an energetic perspective we would say that cultivating that quality of higher consciousness, that emotion called love, strengthens one's intuitive connection to the truth. So the more one loves and the more one is able to forgive oneself and those around one, the less one is hooked into *Apophis*, the illusion. You are freed by your own choice and that is the key: *You are freed by yourself.*

As we have said previously, the more love that you can generate within yourself, for yourself and others, the greater the healing. Love sets up a harmonic field that cascades into the actual cells of the body and into other consciousness levels of one's being. This love is the one thing that many are striving for, and it is very positive and very effective. By all means continue to do this. Love was the fundamental teaching of Sananda, whom you call Jesus, and also the fundamental teaching of the Buddha. Buddha's pathway was through awareness of the duality called *samsara*, the illusion, and the connection to that which was behind it–love, compassion and awareness.

Virginia: Then you do see some advancement on humanity's part?

Hathors: Yes. What needs to be understood, however, is that the advancement takes place through the individual which then emanates to other individuals, and then has a cascading affect so that more and more people awaken. The purpose of the awakening process is to involve more and more people...and that is happening. Of course, when you look at what is happening in the world through the eyes of your press, the newspapers, the television news and radio news, you're not getting a report of the real news. You're getting a report of the fundamental perception of this dualistic world. You are not getting a report of what is actually happening, which is a tremendous renaissance of human emotion and creativity that is expressing itself individually. It is also part of a tremendous flux of chaos as this system of the Earth transits to a new level. So the news reports disasters and the horrible things that are occurring but does not often report on, nor is it even aware of for the most part, the miracles of healing–emotional and otherwise–that are taking place in individual humans on this planet.

Virginia: Certainly not at the level that would be most useful.

Hathors: No.

Virginia: Do you have any other thoughts before we close this chapter?

Hathors: Within the sound of your voice are the keys to innumerable worlds.

Chapter 11
Changing Destiny

We want to discuss the question of destiny, because there is great misunderstanding about this. Your destiny is not fixed. It is not something totally predetermined. There are aspects of your destiny calling to you which have been laid out as a pattern, but the patterns are not permanently fixed. These aspects of fate, or destiny, are probabilities and *can be changed*. If you look at your life in terms of a spiral that moves upward (ascension) or downward (devolution), you can see life as either increasing your energy vibration or lowering it. Consciousness goes up and down. It can vacillate like the seesaw previously mentioned. Human experience is such that one can flow upward to very high levels of awareness and mastery, and one can also spiral downward into lesser levels of awareness.

The question of your destiny and the changing of it depends on your awareness, choice, and vibration. You must have enough awareness to realize that you have a choice. If you practice the methods we have given in this book, you will find your awareness being elevated, so you realize quite fervently that you do have choices in all things. Once you have elevated your awareness to the realization that you are not merely a pawn or a victim in life–but that you have options–the future is made free, open, and malleable to change. This shifted perception is the key to changing your so-called destiny.

When you can accept that the outward patterns

unfolding in your life are the expression of previous patterns held in consciousness, freedom is at hand. These patterns are the fruition of beliefs planted by you, your parents and family, your teachers, your peers and many others in your society. While some of these beliefs seem locked into place, they can be changed, and only you can change those beliefs held inside yourself. There is a tendency for humans to look at difficult situations and feel sorry for themselves because the situations are not going the way they would wish. This is a lost opportunity from our perspective, because if something is not going the way you want and you experience a strong emotional reaction, then the power of that dissatisfaction can be used constructively.

What could be done is to become fully and consciously aware of the incidents and events that are actually occurring–notice the emotional response in yourself to them–and remember that you have a choice in the matter. While you may or may not be able to change the *external situation*, you definitely can change your *internal reaction* to it. By changing your internal reaction to it, you create the pivotal point upon which your destiny will continue to unfold and change.

Let us give a specific example from one of thousands that could be drawn from your daily life. Let's say, hypothetically, that you have begun a relationship with someone that you care very much about, but the person is not reciprocating. In fact they are rejecting you and do not want to be with you even though you want to be with them. This is a source of pain because the attachment and the importance that you place upon being with them, creates pain when you cannot have their company. So this sets up a resonance of feeling rejected, being inferior, frustrated–and the list goes on. However, in that moment when you recognize that they are avoiding you, if instead of blaming them or blaming yourself, you would simply rest in awareness of the fullness of the experience, the pain is alleviated. Becoming aware of their withdrawal from you–aware of your emotional responses, aware of the truth that you have choices in the matter–allows you to choose to experience this situation in a different way–in many different ways.

The way you choose to experience an event will determine how destiny unfolds from that event forward. Indeed, reactions within yourself become an expression of internal mechanisms brought into outer manifestation. The seeds of your future are being planted by you in every moment, in every reaction, with or without awareness. It is simply that *with* awareness you can have some positive effect on the outcome and positively affect destiny. Then, in our example, this hypothetical person who has rejected you, and your reactions to this rejection, are two different things. You have a wide range of choices as to *how* you will experience it. However, we note in humans that there is a tendency to experience new events based on past experience. You might, for instance, have a pattern of expecting rejection, feeling frustrated, blaming and the like. This pattern would then tend to recreate your negative thoughts and emotional reactions *ad nauseum*. Fortunately, there is another way!

As we said, there are many ways to experience any event or experience in your life. What we suggest you seriously consider as a response is what we call *"the highest expression of choice."* By the highest expression of choice we mean identifying that internal alignment or attitude within yourself that allows you the greatest level of awareness, the greatest level of choice, and the highest level of vibratory resonance with your unfolding destiny.

The highest choice has to do with what you would call, in your language, the use of compassion. It is the understanding that no matter what happens to you, you can still hold the attitude of compassion, which has the resonance of acceptance–acceptance of the other person's or the other group of people's response–and an acceptance of your own response. In compassion you are coming from an understanding that all are evolving to the best of their capabilities at any given moment. It is the understanding that people make what appears to be the best choices for themselves or they make what appears to be very bad choices for themselves. Nonetheless, that choice-making is their free will, just as you have your free will. So in those moments of your frustration, sadness, anger, blame, or whatever arises within you–the attitude of compassion allows you to shift those emotional responses inside yourself to an attitude of acceptance.

Then a quite remarkable thing happens. As you hold your own negative emotional responses to whatever is occurring in your life with a healthy acceptance, they will begin to shift and dissipate their energy. The clarity of awareness will return to you as you remember that you have choices! By holding yourself and others in compassion you then raise your own vibratory field, which is the next key to the changing of destiny.

Compassion is a doorway by which one can reach and move into these elevated states of vibratory resonance and from which one's destiny is altered in a most profound and beautiful way. Again the key to all of it occurs in every instant of your life, from moment to moment, from interaction to interaction. Every moment is a choice of how you will respond to what is happening outside yourself or inside yourself. If you "buy into," to use a phrase of your language, your own emotional reactions, then you are buying into the perpetuation of a destiny pattern that may not serve you. Many counselors and psychologists have explained this to you, as have all the great spiritual masters and teachers. Still it bears repeating. When you choose awareness, acceptance and compassion for every life event you experience, that choice brings wisdom and peace as its reward.

Recognize that all beings are evolving and are making the best possible choices for themselves that they presently can. Some people's choices may create pain for you or them, just as some of your own choices may create pain for you or them. Yet by holding life in this paradox of compassion and acceptance, you allow these strong emotional reactions to dissipate and to smooth-out faster, bringing the clarity of awareness. Since nothing is fixed or static–but ever-changing–your new perception shifts your vibration into a higher vibratory field, giving you access to the unfolding higher destiny you seek.

So these are the three keys to unfolding destiny and to changing destiny:

- *awareness*
- *choice*
- *vibration*

There is a phrase that was quoted in your Christian scriptures from the words of Jesus when he said, "To him who has, it shall be given; to him who has not, it shall be taken away." What he is alluding to here is the universal law of vibration. If you want to unfold something, to experience something in your destiny, you must hold it in a vibration of your own consciousness. You must have the feeling of it in order for it to express itself. If you do not have the feeling or the vibration of it, then it cannot express.

If you want loving relationships, then you must hold that vibration of loving relationships in your own consciousness and then you will draw to you, through the laws of magnetics, loving people. If you do not at this moment have loving relationships but are instead experiencing frustration, anger, separation, and isolation, then you must own and accept the truth that you are holding a negative vibration and this is what you are drawing to you through the laws of magnetics. So you must change your thinking and emotional misperceptions to change your vibration. Vibration is a key to changing destiny– the final key that unlocks the doorways to greater perception, greater life, greater rewards.

The power is in your hands, and as we said, there are three aspects of higher consciousness to learn. You must retain the awareness that choice is possible in every circumstance! Indeed, there are certain states of consciousness in which one is not aware of choice, one simply feels choiceless, even hopeless. We would say that some of you who read this material may find yourself in a situation that feels completely hopeless to you, where you cannot fathom or imagine any way out of it. Yet be very clear on this–*the keys to changing your future external reality come from the choices that you make within yourself.* No matter how desperate a situation is, you can change your internal orientation and plant the seeds of a new destiny pattern which will unfold as surely as the sun will rise! So the first key is awareness of choice and the second key is to actually make the choice.

Humans sometimes have a problem with making the choice. We observe many who would rather mope around and be lost in negativity, blaming others or themselves or their past for what is happening to them, rather than making the choice to get out of it. This is simply the expression of a physical law called "entropy" which expresses through your personal energy as lethargy, the reluctance to move. We would say to you that if you are not willing to move, then you are not within the stream of life–for life is always moving and always changing. Once you have awareness of choice, you actually have to *make* the internal choice of how you will evaluate any event or experience that is occurring to you.

From our experience, the most fruitful choice that can be made is what we mentioned earlier as the "highest expression of choice," which comes through the attitude of compassion. Holding both yourself and the other person in an attitude of acceptance, no matter what may be going on in your thoughts and feelings, sets off a resonance in consciousness, a vibrational field that may touch others and change them. It will certainly change you! As you hold that compassion and acceptance, eventually the emotional energies will begin to even out and awareness and clarity of your ability to make positive choices will emerge. Then you will have entered another vibratory resonance, or what might be called an "ascended attitude." And this is your third key! This ascended attitude of acceptance and forgiveness of yourself and all other beings carries a truly high vibration allowing different choices and outcomes than you could achieve in lower vibrations.

Because the laws of the Universe are impersonal and exact, the choices you make daily from moment to moment, are the template of your future destiny. The seeds that you plant in ascended states of awareness and feeling, such as compassion and acceptance, will support your life and your advancing consciousness. Indeed, these seeds of ascension have innumerable outcomes, variable circumstances and even different destinies.

We would remind you once again, friends on Earth, that *you hold within your own hands*, as a metaphor, three keys to your freedom, your elevation and your own evolution. They are:
- *The awareness that you always have choices.*
- *The ability to energize choices.*
- *The constant potential of achieving a new and higher vibration.*

You are the choice maker. And no one else can make your choices for you no matter how difficult your situation may be. By opening your heart to love, however, you can always make a higher choice within yourself that leads to peace. Although you may not be able to affect the external events of your life at every moment, you can change your internal orientation, which will give you the new perspectives that generate exciting choices and a more masterful human destiny.

We see how you hold within yourself all vibrations, from the lowest of the low to the highest and most exalted. You may express the demonic and the bestial–you may express the celestial and the angelic–and everything in between. This is your nature; spiritual mastery is the awareness and understanding that your choices determine what will unfold for you.

And now we pause to ask for your questions on this material, Virginia.

Virginia: We have many discussions on this planet about the degree of control we humans have over our lives, particularly over external events and what we call our own personal destiny. In this chapter you have stated "your destiny is not fixed," so this raises the question of *karma*. Is there *karma*? If so, what is it? Let's begin with that.

Hathors: When we said that your destiny is not fixed, what we meant is the course of one's life is determined, in some regard, in terms of direction. However, you can change that by changing your emotional thought and feeling pattern.

There is *karma. Karma* is simply expressing the result of actions that are done in the Universe. All actions have reactions or consequences, and so everything that one does has an effect. *Karmic* results and effects will be very positive when they are the fruits of compassionate and loving acts. Or they can be quite the opposite. *Karma* is simply experiencing the effects of one's thoughts and actions, then, with either positive or negative results. Happily, if one brings into this lifetime a negative *karmic* debt that needs to be transmuted, needs to be addressed, it can be dealt with externally in terms of events and things that might happen "out of the blue." Or it can be dealt with energetically at the subtle realm and simply be transmuted. This is what alchemy and yoga are about. It's the transmutation, the changing, the clearing of negative *karma* energetically in the subtle realms that we especially encourage. Then you don't have to work it out in your external affairs. So there is *karma*. No one is freed from the consequences of their actions. All must be aware of and meet the consequences of what they do in this lifetime or others.

The destiny, however, that unfolds before anyone–their future–is the result of the seeds that are planted right now in this moment. What a person chooses to feel and what a person chooses to experience in terms of one's reaction to the events of one's life carries responsibility. Simply put, what a person chooses to do to in terms of their actions are seeds that will, according to the impersonal law of the Universe, unfold into *karmic* consequences in the future. So that one is literally shaping one's future destiny in this very moment. It is not that destiny is something that passively waits for you. Rather it is created by you in every moment of your life, in every moment you make choices.

Virginia: Thank you. In the same way that we ponder our personal *karma*, our destinies and so forth, we ponder the destiny of nations. Let's take the United States particularly. What do you see in the probabilities for the United States today and perhaps in its relationships to other nations around the world?

Hathors: The *karmic* repercussions for civilizations operate on the same law as it does for individuals. It's just more massive and there are more variables involved because there are so many people. So the destiny for the United States, as with the individual, is not something that hovers off in the future. It is something that citizens are continually creating and shaping in every moment by the decisions that are made as a culture, as a society.

There are threads that run through the current culture which are the fruition of past actions as a country. Although the United States was formed with a vision of very high purpose, very high integrity, and a view of freedom for the individual that has radiated and uplifted the world to a great extent, it has also brought with it many negativities. These are the negativities of greed, violence, and the domination and oppression of cultures and of world situations. Earth history indicates that a culture or civilization cannot hold that position indefinitely.

One of the things occurring today as a disturbance in the culture, even the breakdown of society, is partly the result of the higher vibratory increases taking place. But it is also a result of the *karmic* seeds, or debts, being repaid by present generations for the negative *karmic* choices of the past. Decisions and actions made as a culture, as a society, since the conception of this country through its various periods of violence and oppression of other people, must be balanced. Because those negativities must be balanced, healed, and a more loving attitude acquired, a very complex phenomenon is going on. The United States is paying its *karmic* debts, as all societies are, but the destiny for this particular country remains to be seen because it will be based on the choices its citizens make day by day. You are creating a legacy for your children and the children of those children, and so forth, who will deal with the consequences of choices taken now.

Virginia: Then what probability do you see for a more compassionate and harmonious relationship among all great nations?

Hathors: Each nation is in the current mind-set of human race consciousness. Nations are operating very much like individuals: territorial, possessive, and looking out for their own interests. There is not yet an understanding in human race consciousness that one can take care of oneself while also being sensitive to the needs of another. Consequently, countries are in various states of evolution, and there is no solid heartfelt international understanding. Those countries that are benevolent to others with their resources are obviously expressing a higher ideal than those countries who have resources and will not share them.

There is a volatile state of affairs within the former Soviet Union presently because no equilibrium has been established. The struggle between those aspects of consciousness that want to free the individual and allow a greater personal expression are in polar opposition to forces that want to suppress the individual and bring society back to a high level of control. A similar situation may develop in China.

Because there are warring elements in consciousness that have not been refined or purified in many of the nations of this world, one could say that war is not going to end in any foreseeable future. What we can say from our perspective, however, is that individuals are waking up all over this planet in every society, and in all levels and positions of those societies. As more and more individuals wake up and recognize that certain things are not tolerable—that they simply cannot do things the way they did them before—and as these awakening people include individuals of power and influence, you will see societies beginning to shift. It is starting; but right now it is figuratively a tug-of-war between many of the forces and factions at all levels of societies throughout the entire world.

Virginia: Continuing that thought, do you have any comment about how to influence a greater destiny in these societies? What can we do as people within them?

Hathors: Societies are an unusual construct or structure, and if persons wish to influence society, it has been almost a set rule that the level of society you operate in determines the effect you will have. So those who have influence and are in levels of power and decision-making have had a greater impact on the machinery of society, the institutions. Individuals who have vision and personal power who are not part of the structure or the mechanism of the institutions, however, can still have a tremendous impact through the virtue of their vision and their power. As they become highly visible, a social mission develops, and that is what is required.

For the average person who feels like they are unable to affect a change because they are not at the level of decision-making, we would say that they are in a place of power if they truly understand their nature in the realm of consciousness, vibration, and resonance. As a person holds a certain frequency or vibration, an emotional tone or emotional signature of peace or love–love in caring for those around them–it will set up a vibratory field that is contagious. Then others who are waking up will also begin to do the same thing. And when you have enough individuals holding a vibration, whether it be fear or whether it be love, then you have a powerful effect on that society. And so it comes down to the fact, although it seems paradoxical, that *the individual* holds the key to how to change society just by positive relationships with self and others.

Virginia: In the same way there are personal and national *karmic* patterns, could you comment on destinies in our solar system and with places beyond our solar system? What *karmas* are we working out there, and how we are doing with all of that?

Hathors: This is a very complex question because you have so many streams or lineages present on this planet and not all who are here on this planet physically are human even though they look human. This is an odd thing to consider. In terms of the *karmic* laws of the Universe which are impersonal, all civilizations–whether galactic or terrestrial–have to work out their *karma*. So there are multiple levels of *karma* being worked out throughout this solar system, galaxy and Universe. It is so complex that we almost would not wish to comment on it because it would take up too much time and would not serve the individual. However, we can say that what is happening on this planet at this time is absolutely unique in intergalactic history. It has never occurred before exactly like it is occurring here and now. Consequently, as this planet goes up in frequency and all beings on it also go through that higher portal, *karmic* debts are being paid at a very rapid pace!

The observers from other realms are therefore looking at this situation with interest to see how fast *karma* is being balanced and how gentle or how violent that balancing is. It is of extreme interest to the observers who realize that the law of *karma* is a set, impersonal law of the Universe. And where better to learn its pattern than here on Earth, where a hotbed of activity is occurring on many levels with the rapid paying and redeeming of *karma*. As *karma* is cleared, destiny can change; and so, in that regard, Earth is a focal point of intense *karmic* activity at the moment.

Virginia: Since you've discussed humanity's shift into higher consciousness, could you comment on whether, as Earth's consciousness shifts into higher frequency, the planet will remain in the same physical location in the solar system? Or, as some people have indicated, is there to be a movement out of its present physical location?

Hathors: No one knows for sure what is going to happen. That is why there is so much observation taking place. There are theories from our scientists, of course, and from scientists in other cultures and civilizations who have actually met and talked about this extensively. Two theories about this are predominant at the moment. One is that the Earth will literally move its physical location in the solar system. And the other theory is that it's going to stay physically in the same location but vibrationally it will be in a different dimension. This is the one that our group tends to feel will take place. However, the entire solar system, the Universe, and all the galaxies within the Universe are all presently moving towards one central point within the Universe, so in that sense enormous movement is occurring right now. Because the movement is occurring now you will see an acceleration of that movement in the galaxies. As to Earth's relationship in the solar system, what will happen is not clear to us at this time. There are too many variables.

Virginia: You know in our Earth history that we have

prophecies from the Book of Revelations in the Bible, from the Hopi nation, and from many other historical sources and living individuals that speak of certain destiny factors that will play out. Can you comment upon the term "prophecy" and whether it has had value, and is presently having value, here on our planet?

Hathors: Prophecy is a capacity of consciousness to predict the future based on an understanding of what is happening energetically at the moment. So it's like mapping out a course of destiny based on an understanding that changes can occur. The danger in prophecy is that it is taken as *a fact* rather than *a probability* by many people who receive it. Thus the predictions and prophecies of Earth disasters are creating extreme anxiety in many individuals because they are interpreting the prophecy as fact and this is a misconception.

Prophecy is a probability. It's an understanding of what might happen if the course of events continues to unfold the way it is going now. For instance, if a person has a shoe that does not fit them, and they continue walking until pain and irritation are felt, then there could be a prophecy that a blister will result. If one interprets that as fact, without choice, then one will not take off the shoe. One could then say to themselves, perhaps, that the blister was pre-ordained–that "I had no choice in the matter."

Unfortunately, we see something like this occurring among those who are prophesying Earth disasters. From our perspective, from our understanding, nothing in terms of Earth changes are absolute. They are probabilities that may or may not occur, based upon what happens with human consciousness and Earth consciousness. Do not receive prophecies as fact when you hear them, but as probabilities. It is true that there are Earth changes because the Earth is evolving and so are you. But the Earth changes do not have to be as cataclysmic as many are reporting.

The true function of prophecy is to warn the society

and the individual that this is probably what lies ahead. The prophet points to the future destiny and says, this is where we are heading. Do we want to continue on the path we are taking? That is the true function of prophecy. It is not to say that what we see in the prophetic vision is what will occur and there is no choice. That is error, according to our understanding.

Virginia: We presently have many discussions about time, the measurement of time, the acceleration of time, the Mayan calendar concept and so forth. How does the measurement of time relate to destiny?

Hathors: You have opened up a very large topic here. And it may take quite a while to explain this, but we will try to be succinct. It is related to language, as odd as that seems. When you have an experience and you describe that experience through language, you are better able to grasp the experience–to hold it. And language facilitates the recognition of experience. One can certainly have experience without language, but *language allows consciousness to mark an experience*. For example, if you try to remember something that has occurred in the past– let's say that you put a book in a drawer and you leave the house and you go somewhere across town. Then you realize that you need the book so you call home to your partner, tell them you put the book in the second drawer, and ask them to read you a particular page. Language has assisted you to communicate, so language allows the facilitation of experience (until you become telepathic again). It would be very difficult at present to direct the person to the book if you did not have language. So language charts a pathway through experience and it is the function of language to do so, but it is also its limitation, we might add.

Time is a similar process. It is an actual flow but it is much more complex than the linear way your society, your culture, measures it. Because time is actually spiraling and non-linear, it is multi-dimensional in nature, not three-dimensional. Please realize that as soon as you use a linear measure of time, or any system of measurement, you have created an effect upon perception. Now–there are three particular qualities or levels of time about which we would like to speak.

The first quality would be *biological time*–the organic time, the rhythms of your body, the rhythm of your breath, the rhythm of the pulse of your heart, the rhythm of the wind, the rhythms of the water on this Earth–this would all be related to Earth rhythms and the biological rhythms of your body that are organic. You also have the clock, which was invented to measure time sequentially in bits and pieces, so that whole societies of humans live their lives according to a mechanistic measurement of time, not according to their biological wisdom. This is creating tremendous stress on individuals, which is not fully recognized. Living one's life by the clock in order to fit into the convenience of society may serve you at one level, but at a biological level it is very stressful because it disconnects you from your biological wisdom!

Measuring out time biologically according to the rhythms of nature brings us to the second level of time which is connected to the moon. *The lunar sequence of time*–the thirteen full moons that pass within roughly a year's time–is a more organic, a truer measure of time than the current Gregorian calendar used by many world societies–especially Western societies. The 12-month Gregorian calendar was created to disconnect people from the lunar, organic sense of time. The creators of the calendar were very precise in what they were doing. It was a "rip off," to use a street term on your planet. It disconnects! It was a way to pull human consciousness out of the Great Mother awareness of Earth and connect it to something that was abstract. So, when one measures time using the Gregorian calendar, one is literally out of synchronization with the true flow of time. It's an arbitrary measurement. It was pulled out of the hat, so to speak. It is not organic. It does not reflect the rhythms of the body nor does it reflect the rhythms of Earth. So a truer sense of time would be to return to the lunar phases.

And finally, the third sense of time is *intergalactic*, which is the flow and relationships of galaxies to one another with reference to the Great Central Sun and their relationships to your Sun, the star of this solar system. That is another level of time about which you know very little. So you have three levels of true time: (1) *Biological*, (2) *Lunar*, and (3) *Intergalactic*.

One can measure time sequentially–mechanistically–and seemingly begin to have a control over Earth, because one can actually make things happen according to time. And this is true because one is creating another time stream through consciousness. But what we would say to you is, if you wish to come into an accurate description of time that is aligned with the Universe, then turn your attention away from the clock and the calendar as you use it, and turn it towards your body, towards the Moon and the Sun.

Virginia: Is the Mayan calendar capable of doing that for us?

Hathors: The Mayan calendar is capable of tracking the lunar phases and the intergalactic phases. It does not track the body wisdom. The body wisdom is an organic, biological measurement of time that is held within the individual. But yes, for the lunar phases and intergalactic time, the Mayan calendar is the most accurate descriptor that you have in your possession.

Virginia: Then what is our best way to use time given this dichotomy of the present society?

Hathors: Unless you "drop out", as it were, you will have to find a balance. If you have to adjust to society–and most individuals do–then you may have to pay homage to the clock and be where you agree to be at a certain hour. But while you are following the clock, pay attention to your own body. Perhaps when everyone else is eating may not be your time to eat. Maybe it is a time to rest, to read or to take a walk, and then eat something later.

The differences in the rhythms of individuals are vast. So you must become sensitive to your own rhythms and take care to make choices from your body wisdom while also paying attention to the clock and the Gregorian calendar. We would simply encourage you to begin to pay attention to the lunar phases and to begin to sense that movement of time from the new moon to the next new moon. If you can live in two worlds, you can be in society, noticing and tracking things according to that measurement, and at the same time be aware of and live your life in these deeper natural rhythms.

Virginia: You said earlier that there were secret geometries. Could you discuss those geometries we often talk about, such as the "Flower of Life," and various mathematical understandings and rituals? Do you see that these have affected destiny or are affecting our destiny now?

Hathors: The Flower of Life is a fundamental pattern that the Universe is laid out on, so even the molecular and atomic grids are laid out in this pattern; therefore, it's the platform that unfolds destiny. It is the blueprint. Without it there would be no manifestation. But is your question, "Has an awareness of this pattern affected destiny?"

Virginia: Yes.

Hathors: As more people recognize the hermetic truth "As above, so below"—that all things are interconnected—one begins to come out of the miasma of the belief that things are random. To recognize that things are connected and there is an intelligence that holds all things together is wisdom. As one awakens to that truth, destiny is changed because one cannot continue to do things that one did when one was asleep. So yes, it is serving the purpose of waking up and changing individual and collective destinies.

Virginia: Could you please comment about any prior

civilization on the planet which really understood its destiny and attained a high degree of achievement with it?

Hathors: Lemuria was capable of this for an extended time. Atlantis did this for a while until they made an error in perception and got into duality as their reality–until they became so mental that they lost the balance of love. Of course, the high destiny of the golden period of Egypt and the golden period of Greece were all a tremendous flowering and forward movement in human consciousness. There were also cultures in Africa for which you have no names because your history does not mark them.

As stated, we have had prior relationships with many early civilizations. Because of our intense relationship with the high period of the Egyptian flowering, we know the powerful seeds of influence and achievement that were gained then; especially through the Mystery Schools and the multi-faceted use of the Rods of Power.

Virginia: Rods of Power? Could you clarify this term?

Hathors: (...pausing to discuss the question among themselves...) Excuse the delay, but we were pondering how much to say about this topic, since to adequately answer would be quite lengthy. We expect it would make this chapter too long and ask whether you wish us to continue or not?

Virginia: To avoid missing anything important, why don't we complete this chapter now and carry the Rods of Power topic forward?

Hathors: Agreed. Then let us complete our remarks with a final reminder that your destiny is not totally predetermined, but rests in the potential probabilities of higher consciousness. Through this elevated awareness, your positive choices, and your loving vibratory frequency, you are on an expanding journey of cosmic proportions.

By using the Self-Mastery Exercises we've recommended for your growth and healing, you will affect far more than your own life, and Earth's, progress. You will assist in bringing light and hope to many other beings presently unknown to you.

Chapter 12
Rods of Power

The term "Rods of Power" can refer to four concepts, the first of which was the use of actual physical metal rods by ancient Egyptians in their temples and Mystery Schools. You will see, in some of the hieroglyphic paintings, rods that have another rod that is curled up. Sometimes there is an *ankh* placed at the top of the rod. These rods were used to specifically activate *chakras*, (energy centers or vortices), within the body of the initiate. The rods would be placed along an initiate's back and then struck, causing the rods to sound much like a tuning fork, thus creating resonant patterns of sound that would go into the spine and activate the *chakras*. These rods were of different lengths and when used in a specific manner, a specific sequence, they caused the life-force, the *Sekhem*– the power of consciousness as it expresses itself through physicality–to rise up. This life-force would rise up the spine and activate different *chakras* and centers. And so the Rods of Power were used to assist the initiate to enter these higher realms of consciousness and then to explore those worlds.

The second meaning of Rods of Power has to do with the actual energy flows that exist within the human body. The central understanding of this has to do with what is called the *pranic* tube or the central column–which is that tube-like structure that you have worked with in previous exercises. This *pranic* tube is a powerful focal point for self-evolution, and there are specific energy flows that run from each of the *chakras* to the other *chakras* within this tube. For instance, you could have an energy movement or relationship from the sexual center to the heart or to the power center. If the energy flow or rod that connects the second *chakra* (sexual center) to the power center is activated, then sex will be expressed as a means to achieve power. However, if one were to express sexuality through the heart, which is a higher frequency range, then the rod or the connecting flows between the sexual center and the heart would be activated...and so forth up the spine.

In this way, the Rods of Power also refer to energy relationships between different frequency ranges of one's own experience. So while the Rods of Power in the first sense are physically activated externally by someone who understands how to use the rods to move these energies, the second sense of the term involves energy systems within your own domain of choice and intuition. Thus, if you are acting with the highest possible intention, you will activate those Rods of Power that connect you to the higher centers (*chakras*). This is a way that you can "bootstrap," to use a computer term, and raise yourself up in consciousness through intentionality.

For example, if you have a sexual relationship coming from a place of love rather than a place of pure power, you can elevate the frequency range so that sex can be an avenue, a means, for touching into the higher frequency domains of your own consciousness. If you move into sexual expression with a desire to have clarity and a connection to the highest aspects of your own being, then you will activate your crown center, relate it to the sex center, and not have to make a choice between one or the other. Instead, you can have several energy flows going simultaneously. The point here is that through the power of your intention and choice—and how you approach the activities in your life—you can determine which rods or energy flows will be activated within that *pranic* tube.

There is also a third meaning of the term Rods of Power which we would like to explain–and it, too, refers to a physical rod or staff used in ancient Egypt in the times of the high initiates. At the top of this type of rod was a cluster of specific crystals and gems whose frequency and structure amplified the thoughts that emanated out of the initiate's third eye. This occurred when the rod or the staff was held at arms length directly in front of the initiate with the crystals lined up in a direct line with the third eye. The initiate, using inner methods, could formulate a thought and direct it into the crystals, which would amplify that particular thought.

The rod was a very powerful and very effective tool–and at the same time quite dangerous–so it is not something that we wish to go into any further because this technology was used and misused in a different form in the time of Atlantis. It was altered when it came into Egypt. However, the fundamental understanding of how crystals can be used to amplify thought energies for healing are essentially the same even today.

There is a fourth and final understanding about the term Rods of Power which we would like to address now and it has to do with what might be termed the "fourth state of awareness." But before we discuss this fourth state of awareness, let us review the first three states of awareness, in case you are not familiar with them.

The *first state of awareness* is *vegetative* awareness, meaning that as a human being you do not exist as self-concept; only your body exists. Notice an infant when it is first born. The body merely has an internal awareness of itself and a need to keep functioning. In similar fashion, a person who may have suffered a massive stroke and lost all functioning within the higher brain centers retains no memory of self, even though the body would continue functioning if the vital organs were not damaged and the primitive structures of the brain were intact. So this first level of awareness is where the body is aware of itself and continues its functioning.

The *second state of awareness* is *self-awareness* where one moves out of the vegetative state, or what you might call the lower animal state, into an awareness of self or consciousness as part of the matrix of physicality–yet separate from it. In the higher states of such an awareness–in what the ancients called being "the witness"–one watches oneself while being aware of oneself. This awareness is part of the continuum of biological functioning and yet is separate from it, as well. So this self-awareness is the second state or second level of awareness and it grows by watching one's emotions, one's drives, one's instincts, and one's thoughts.

The *third state of awareness* concerns others in the *external world*. It involves awareness of other people, other relationships, the external world, and the forces of which one is a part. Indeed, navigating oneself through these various forces and relationships is considered a part of normal human existence. Since society and its laws are based upon a conscious recognition of this third level of awareness, and an agreement upon what is required within that level of awareness, it constitutes a major life activity. This level is where most humans stop in their development.

There is a *fourth state of awareness*, however, which is a movement in consciousness from the personal into the *transpersonal* realm. There are levels even beyond that, but they are so abstract as to be useless for most people. This shift into transpersonal experience is the next evolutionary stage for humanity. Our understanding of this fourth level of awareness is that it brings the understanding that all life is living itself and expressing itself through you. As stated, it is a movement from the personal into the transpersonal. It is a movement from the egocentric into the universal. It is a movement in which one's awareness shifts and one becomes very clear that life is expressing itself in multitudinous forms. Life is moving through rain forests, moving through oceans, moving through chimpanzees, through dogs, through goldfish, through amoebas, through dolphins and whales, and in the tiniest seeds that are blown on the wind. It is also expressing a deep understanding through you as a human that your humanness, while sacred, is no more important than any other form through which life is expressing its vastness. And so this fourth level of awareness is a profoundly spiritual context in which one's own life role continues and one's experience of oneself, the world, and life is vastly and forever different.

Much of the inner teachings of the Mystery Schools and the understanding of the initiates was to make that shift into the fourth level of awareness. That fourth level of awareness is activated by many things. It may be activated by altruistic service to others. It may be activated through the heart, through the emotion of love and relationships. It may be activated through an understanding of the Sacred Elements or may be brought about by uplifting the *Ka*. There are many possibilities but the one possibility that extends through all of them is the energy flow in the central column, the *pranic* tube, to which we have referred before.

Specifically, when one begins the movement into the fourth level of awareness, the *pranic* tube becomes activated in a very strong way though one may or may not be aware of it depending on one's sensitivity. However, essentially what happens is that through your body–heaven and Earth meet. The heavenly, celestial forces–which actually have a reality as particles–are actually brought down through the *pranic* tube, through the crown into the heart, and the Earthly forces and energies are brought up into the heart, as well, where they meet. The celestial forces can also meet in each of the vortices or *chakras* of the body. So this *pranic* tube becomes very crucial as one moves into the fourth level of awareness.

Essentially, what happens in the fourth level is that

instead of the various separate rods being activated in their relationship to the different centers, the entire rod or *pranic* tube is activated. When the *pranic* tube begins to vibrate with *pranic* intensity, one has moved out of the personal human into the transpersonal human and one enters the universal life. Here the inter-dimensional worlds open up and reveal themselves and one begins living a very different life. Externally, as you look at such a person you may not see anything radically different from other people, but internally there is a very different reality. It is this understanding of the term Rods of Power that we would like to emphasize and encourage because it is something that is distinctly open as an evolutionary step for everyone. It is simply a matter of choice and intention as to whether you enter that path or not.

And now, Virginia, have you questions to ask?

Virginia: Regarding the relationships and the movements of energy flows between the *chakras* as you've described them here, is this like what we would call a *kundalini* experience or opening? Also, for most humans today, which of the possible *chakra* energy flow patterns are the safest and most beneficial for us to establish? It wasn't clear whether all of these patterns of *chakra* movements begin with, and utilize, the sex or root *chakra* energy in the beginning stage.

Hathors: As to which of the energy centers (*charkas*) would be safest for all people to use, the heart center would be that focal point. The reason for this is that the heart center is the seat of the soul which we call *Ku* and that *Ku*, the soul, is the seed consciousness that sits in the heart center. So focusing the various energy flows and power rods in relationship to the heart is definitely the safest approach, unless one has a totally clear understanding of how to use these very subtle energies. The reason the heart accelerates evolution the fastest for most individuals is that the heart generates the love emotion, the positive feeling state, and the harmonic of unconditional love. When unconditional love becomes one's focal point, then one is moving upwards in terms of the ascending spiral. So, as previously explained, if one has sexual relationships with another human while expressing that love in relationship to the heart, then of course that emotion, that feeling state, will permeate the sexual expression. Then the sexual expression becomes sacred and is elevated.

In the same way, if one expresses the energy relationship between the heart and power center (solar plexus *chakra*), one's expression of power through love elevates the use of power. If one speaks the truth of one's being (through the throat *chakra*) in relationship to the heart, through love, then one's words are elevated and have a benevolent effect. Similarly, if one's vision is opening up clairvoyantly (through the brow *chakra*) and is in a heart-based relationship, then one will see those regions of what you might call the etheric or the astral–subtle realms that are in the vibratory field of the heart. You then bypass the negativity that exists in the astral realm and your perceptions of the subtle realms are elevated. This also occurs with opening the crown *chakra* when one moves into the transpersonal center. So the heart center is the most beneficial focal point in relationship to the other rods–or energy flows–at this time in human development.

The answer to your question as to whether this movement of energy is likened unto the *kundalini* is yes. Understand that there are also other energies that move up the spine besides the *kundalini* energy. However, the initiatory experience in the temples when the rods were used did activate what is called the *kundalini* energy.

This *kundalini*, the electromagnetic energy field of consciousness, is held within the physical body beginning at the root *chakra*. The *kundalini* energy moves up from the spine so all further movement of energy within the body, within the subtle realms, begins at the root. The life force which we call *Sekhem* is held in the stomach area, the solar plexus, and the lower stomach, and then moves down into the sexual organs before moving up the spine. This energy is activated by focusing at the second energy center (the sexual center or sacral *chakra*). So in the use of Egyptian Alchemy, these centers are very important to the foundation of spiritual evolution.

As we understand it, the life-force itself is held in the body and is first expressed as metabolism and then moves down into the root *chakra*–from where the energy flow moves upward. As mentioned, when the heart is a focal point for whatever energy relationship exists between the energy rods, then those energies are elevated through love. We want to be clear that *the vital force of the body and the vital force of consciousness originate in the lower chakras so one does not really bypass them. It's simply that those life-force energies can be expressed through the focus of the heart.*

Virginia: Yes, that does answer the question, thank you. Now in terms of the mechanical rods, the metals ones, which were used in the past Mystery Schools in Egypt, are they passé for us today? Shouldn't we, as you've indicated in this material, look to our own inner resources and not be so involved in external sources? Or am I misunderstanding the message? In other words, should we use those metal Rods of Power today or utilize the practical exercises that you've brought forth? Or is there some combination of these?

Hathors: The use of inner technology and outer technology is ideally one of balance. There is a fascination by humans today with gadgets and external technology, many believing that the external technology will deliver them into higher consciousness without any inner work required. This is fallacy, of course, for the inner is what actually creates the movement. The rods were simply an assist, if you will. The actual movement of the vital force up the spine was created by the initiate's inner intention, focus and will. What the rod did was to gently coax the energy in that movement.

At this point in human evolution, the use of sound, whether created through rods or electronic means, can certainly be an assist. However, it is the inner focus of consciousness that actually creates the energy movement; therefore, while the external technology could be helpful, a vast majority of the flow occurs through inner awareness and mastery. Our focus, our understanding and our belief about this issue is to master one's own inner subtle realms–then one has personal mastery and the external technologies are not needed at all. In our teaching, it is your personal inner mastery that we propose as the ideal.

Virginia: Understood. Could you give us a guesstimate about how many initiates in the Egyptian Mystery Schools earned what we call their ascension mastery using this focus of inner development? And then some comparison with how many people on the planet today are achieving their own inner mastery so we have some idea of how we are doing compared to prior times–the Egyptian period in particular?

Hathors: So you want a percentage of the number of initiates?

Virginia: Yes, something about how many people got their mastery–which I assume was not easy in those times!

Hathors: Mastery is not easy at any time (...said with humor...)! Well, first of all, we do not have the akashic records of all the souls who have gone through the various initiatory processes worldwide because we were concerned with Mystery Schools in one particular area. However, we can speak about Egypt during the period when the Egyptian Mystery Schools were no longer physically present...a time when the bulk of the external teaching had been completed. We do however, acknowledge that some Mystery Schools continued, although they were less accessible and there were fewer and fewer people involved. Probably less than *ten percent* of the initiates achieved mastery, if we consider mastery as the point where one was able to use one's consciousness to ascend to the highest level of being.

Virginia: *Ten percent* of the group that started?

Hathors: Yes.

Virginia: And what percentage of the general population were initiates? A small portion of it?

Hathors: Oh, very small. Less than *one percent* of the total population. What we're saying is that of the general population, less than *one percent* would have dedicated themselves to becoming initiates. There were those who took the outer roles of priest and priestesses, if you understand, but to those who truly chose to be initiates and take that path of soul accomplishment to the highest realms, less than *one percent* of the population was involved. Of those initiates, less than *ten percent* achieved the highest level of what the Mystery School was teaching. *However, it does not mean that the other 90 percent of the initiates failed, because mastery is something that extends through all lifetimes!* This is a misunderstanding that humans currently may believe regarding mastery.

It is untrue that if you don't "make it" in this life you have failed somehow. That is a preposterous belief as we see it because this life is simply one embodiment in time and space and is one expression of the *Ku*, the soul. Indeed, every subsequent lifetime is another expression of your soul. It's like growing petals on a flower. When the petals have been strengthened and are matured sufficiently, then the blossom opens and reaches the final attainment, if you will. *But the process of going there is the mastery.* So we are uncomfortable with saying that *90 percent* of the initiates failed because, in our understanding, they were reaching mastery. It is simply in the timing of things that during one embodiment they did not reach that final attainment to which the Mystery School was leading them. However, subsequent to that, many of them did reach that mastery in other lifetimes after Egypt.

Virginia: I think that clarifies it. Then could you comment about our present situation? I believe that you mentioned elsewhere in the book that today the human family is experiencing their mastery initiations in everyday situations, unlike the former self-identified initiates who went into a specific Mystery School. Could you clarify how this everyday learning experience works for humans today and give an example from an individual's daily life to help us get your point of how we really are moving into mastery day by day?

Hathors: We would like to answer that question using one of the myths of the time of ancient Egypt which is called the Resurrection of *Osiris*. Although the myth is very long and complex it is actually an alchemical key, a map of how to attain the resurrection of consciousness. It is an instruction book or manual, if you will, but it is in code, symbolic code. In the story of *Osiris*, *Osiris* has a brother *Set*, who is a code for the serpent called *Apophis*—the serpent of duality. This serpent of duality simply means that the conflict of good and evil occurs only below the level of Supreme Being which is non-dual, unified, and has no conflict. So there is a part of consciousness that is still balanced, unmoving, in equilibrium, that is omniscient, omnipresent and is eternally at peace.

Yet there is another aspect or level of that consciousness, human consciousness, which is in duality. In the myth the symbol for, or the word for, that which is eternally omnipresent and ever-peaceful is *maat* which is opposite the serpent *Apophis*, or duality. So the story of *Osiris* is the story of the battle, if you will, between *Apophis* and *maat*, between truth and illusion.

In the myth, *Set*, who is the brother of *Osiris*, cuts him into tiny pieces and sends them all over the world. This is the symbol of the duality, the dualistic mind, which cuts things into pieces and scatters them instead of holding the wholeness of things. To be brief, *Osiris* has a son named *Horus* who avenges his death. As *Horus* is the symbol of *maat* whereas *Set* is the symbol of *Apophis*–so *Horus* is the expression of the truth, the omnipresent, the eternal peace and *Set* is the expression of the dualistic nature.

The myth is about the conflict between these two aspects, and in the final understanding of the myth there is a being that emerges called *Set-Horus* where *Set* is joined with *Horus* as one being, although separate. *Horus* is shown in his form as a hawk-headed human and *Set* is shown with a dog-like head on a human form. The alchemical understanding of this is that humans are joined in a co-mixture of illusion and truth. There is the animal nature of *Set* which is fundamentally a reluctance or refusal to forgive and to release anger and jealousy, so these qualities are what make him the demonic one in this mythology. Since *Horus* is the one who is connected to the Divine, there is an aspect of all humans that is both Divine and demonic. What alchemy says, what the myth says, is that you must acknowledge the truth of where you are–that you have parts of you that are unforgiving, jealous, petty, and anger-filled, just as you have parts that are uplifted, loving and compassionate.

The continuing question is, which part will you come from? Which will you choose to express–the *Set* nature or the *Horus* nature? They are both there and they are available at any moment, because life is a continual free-will decision about which you will choose to express. In the Mystery Schools of Egypt, the priests and priestesses would "scan" the initiates to sense where they were coming from in their morality. If an initiate was more *Set*-like than *Horus*-like, meaning they were holding patterns of unforgiveness, jealousy, and anger–then they would not be allowed access to the inner teachings and the inner technologies because it would be dangerous to empower someone who was unbalanced like this.

And so the selection of students was done by the priests and priestesses. It was a responsibility of the guardians of the Mystery School to ascertain the moral quality of the initiates. That process does not exist today in quite the same way because each individual must do that for themselves. Earth is now moving into a higher vibratory field and everything is being stimulated, including both the *Set* nature of individuals and the *Horus* nature. For many humans now, their worst and/or their best natures are coming out as a response to the Earth's movement upwards in vibration. And so your life situations provide an opportunity, whether you are aware of it or not, to make a choice. Will you respond to a situation through your *Set* nature, through anger, through jealousy, through pettiness, through unforgiveness? Or will you choose to respond to the situation from your *Horus* nature which is love and compassion, understanding and truth? Your emotional responses create your destiny and the future patterns that unfold in your life. You lay the road or the pathway to heaven or hell, brick by brick, by the choices you make in your everyday life.

Virginia: Yes, thank you. Continuing with that thought, do you see any way in which human beings today on the planet can begin to gage how they're doing? Obviously, the way their life is working is certainly an example. Is there anything of clarity that you can give about this so that we can assess our own progress?

Hathors: Well, first of all we would say that you cannot ascertain your spiritual progress based on how your life is working *externally*. Some people believe that if they do the "right things," their lives will be perfect. They also believe that if something negative occurs they have failed. This is not our understanding. You have to realize that the situations you encounter in your life are "surface events," meaning that they occur on the surface of awareness (three-dimensional reality, in other words). Underneath the events, themselves, are vast unseen forces operating from deep within consciousness itself. This consciousness may be expressing through you, through your culture, through Earth changes and even through cosmic forces of unimaginable proportions. Not all events are created solely by you (though your perception of them most assuredly is). These various forces–individual, cultural, Earth-based, and cosmic–interact to create the surface events of your destiny.

Some of these forces manifesting in your life are the results of thoughts, feelings, and actions on your part. They are seeds you have planted in the soil of your own consciousness. Some of these may be recent, meaning within the scope of your present life, while others may have a more ancient origin. Time is not a hindrance here. Thoughts or actions entertained in other lifetimes can have their *karmic* effect in your present life. This is not a punishment, but an opportunity for the soul to recognize the fruits of its actions.

To the advancing or ascending soul, life events are seen as wondrous and beautiful things for they afford the possibility of healing, and healing the past is crucial to the ascension of consciousness. Therefore, whatever events unfold in your life, embrace them with awareness, compassion and intelligent choice. Don't decry your fate. Accept what happens, not as a kind of resignation or "giving in," but rather as an acknowledgment of what is actually occurring. From this "owning" or acceptance of your situation you can move to change those things which are in your power to change.

This attitude of acceptance will then enable you to elevate yourself through the harmonic of self-love and right action, thereby planting the seeds of higher destiny and greater spiritual power.

Chapter 13
The Unasked Question

Our final topic is entitled "The Unasked Question" because, when moving through and exploring realms of consciousness and the potential for higher consciousness, you'll find that the questions you ask determine the answers you receive. Because the answers are embedded in the questions themselves, it is crucial to ask the correct questions so that the answers of greatest benefit will reveal themselves to you. As we look at the evolutionary patterns of human beings, it appears obvious that most are involved with their own little world, their own desires, their own wishes, the fulfillment of their own personal fantasies. Each person seems to be striking out on his/her own, so to speak. Therefore, the question that most individuals ask is, "What will I get out of this?"

In nearly every situation that presents itself, most people ask the question, "What's in it for me?" And so that is their primary filtering. A few humans have grown beyond this attitude, or course, which is encouraging. Yet the masses are still unconscious in many ways. While "What's in it for me?" is appropriate for certain levels of evolution, it is too restrictive for the higher levels of consciousness presently within your grasp.

Friends, the unasked question is a question whose answer will bring you the greatest freedom, the greatest acceleration of growth, the greatest expansion of awareness, and the greatest mastery of your own consciousness. The answers to some of life's deepest, most profound mysteries lie within this major question. The context for this question comes from the realization that one is part of an ongoing greater life experience. Life is living itself and presently expressing itself through multitudinous forms, including you.

The tree, for example, has one primary life-force moving through it that expresses through hundreds, even thousands of leaves. Although each leaf is important to the tree, the tree is far beyond any of its individual leaves. Indeed, the consciousness of a leaf cannot hold the consciousness of the tree since the tree is vaster than the leaf that hangs from one of its boughs. And yet paradoxically, at the deepest level of matter and consciousness, the tree is also embedded in the leaf as information.

The vast number of neurons within your brain are interconnected, allowing the flows of information that may be viewed as multitudes of individual consciousnesses, for indeed that is what they are. Each neuron holds its own awareness of itself and yet links with others. That linking with others is what creates the phenomenon of your consciousness, your conscious awareness in the body. The individual neuron within your brain does not have an awareness of the vast complexity of which it is a part. This is true with you, also. The multitudinous beings on this planet, be they human, plant, or animal, are all parts of a greater life–the expressions of a greater mind, if you will.

Yes, you are as neurons to the Earth. Consequently, the question that most humans ask, "What is in this for me? What is of value for me personally in any given situation, in any given encounter?" only perpetuates answers which are by their nature very restrictive. By shifting the awareness of your own needs and desires to the unasked question, "What can I do for the greater good in this situation?" your consciousness evolves. You see, the context has radically shifted, hasn't it? For now, rather than being focused and constricted only on your own individual needs, you have deliberately chosen to extend yourself to the collective expression of life in its multiple forms.

It has been said that if you wish to be loved you must love, which is an aspect of the question we are discussing. If you wish to experience being loved, then extend the energy of love to someone else. In letting your love flow out to others, through the law of magnetics and resonance, love will respond and return back to you. But you must extend yourself beyond your own tiny world of beliefs, reactions, and desires to use this wonderful law. Extending your awareness to assist others when possible, not at your own expense but in a balanced, integrated way, allows your individual awareness to expand into the greater whole. This occurs when you become aware of what is expressing itself all around you and not just through you.

It is as if an individual neuron within your brain were to transform itself and become aware of the totality of the galaxy of neurons within the entirety of the brain. This is a tremendous shift in focus, and is what the unasked question will open for you if you begin to approach your life in service to life. *Living your life in service to life* is a different context than living your life just for yourself. Living your life for life, for the expression of life, as it moves through you and others, will lead you to make choices for yourself and choices in your interactions with others—choices that affirm life, expand it, cherish it, and hold all other beings as sacred. When one begins this process of moving into living one's life for the benefit of life itself, one has entered a greater sea of possibilities, a greater ocean of opportunity. Life becomes much richer, much more fulfilling, because one begins to see the interconnectedness of all things and the vast powers of consciousness that move through the Universe. Once placed in its embrace—one sees, feels and experiences one's own life as sacred—and all other lives as sacred, too.

Thus, although we have come to encourage and assist you, it is appropriate that we should leave you with a challenge. We challenge you to take this opportunity that you have right before you to live your life in service to life itself. This does not mean giving away your power to anyone else. This does not mean taking care of anyone at your own expense. This means being aware of the interconnectedness of all things, honoring all beings so that the motivation for one's actions become not merely self-interest but interest in the greater good. As you continue to evolve and move up through the spiral of ascension, through the spiral of consciousness, your perspective of the collective good will change, for all things are relative to the state of consciousness through which you perceive it. This is a crucial concept! Do remember, please, that *all things are relative to the state of consciousness through which they are perceived.* So what might seem like a negative situation at one level of consciousness can actually be experienced as positive in another state of consciousness.

Nothing is binding or absolute in the relative Universe in which you live. The only thing which is absolute and unchanging is the deepest unmoving center of your own consciousness. As you begin to align yourself with the evolution of life itself, with the growth of life and consciousness, you will be lifted up in a way that you may not be able to imagine. For miracles occur! Opportunities open and your destiny is changed when you live in service to life. Why? This vibration changes all things in the twinkling of an eye. The past can be changed and the future opened with possibilities beyond imagination. And so we challenge you to live and experiment just as many saints, teachers, and masters have done previously—and are currently doing. Try it for a few weeks and see what happens. When there is an opportunity to be kind to another human or an animal, let your kindness show. When there is an opportunity to show compassion to another, be compassionate.

When there is an opportunity to listen to someone,

grant the grace and listen. Listen fully and deeply without wanting to impose your own views, your own agendas. As you listen to hear and receive the other, you will see your relationships being vastly and quickly transformed. There are miracles waiting for you when you ask the unasked question, "*What can I do here that will serve the greater good? What can I do here that will serve life's deepest purpose through me?*"

Finally, we would say to you that you hold the keys to your own liberation, to your own enlightenment, to your own upliftment. These keys are obtained through the power of your awareness, your ability to make choices, and the law of vibration and resonance. The law assures that whatever you resonate to will be revealed to you. If your consciousness resonates with the highest of the high, you will experience life in an exalted celestial way. If you experience your life through the vibration of conflict and greed and constricted awareness then you will experience life as a kind of hell. All of these domains and realms exist simultaneously and can be activated by you at any moment. In fact, they are activated by you every moment of your life through the act of choice.

While living your life in service to the greater life, to the evolution of consciousness as it expresses through you, you assure yourself a secure footing on the stairway that leads to the heavenly realms. Whatever choice you make, acknowledge your mastery and your freedom to express it. To those of you who have already chosen, or who now choose to serve life and the growth of consciousness as it expresses through you and all beings, we welcome you as brothers and sisters on the journey. So be it.

And now once again, Virginia, we do invite you to ask your questions.

Virginia: You've indicated that all things are relative to the state of consciousness through which they are perceived. What would be our highest state of consciousness to hold in relationship to you, the Hathors, as we receive information from you or other spiritual beings during this time of awakening?

Hathors: The highest state of consciousness through which we may be truly perceived, as we understand it, is the vibrational field that you call love. This is not an indiscriminate love; it's not loving without awareness of those things that are out of alignment, but uses discrimination as an important part of awareness. It is simply that from that vibratory place of love within yourself, you are able to perceive things more clearly in terms of their true nature, as opposed to what your senses are telling you.

The physical senses are giving you one piece of information, but it's only a very small sliver of what is occurring. However, if you come from an attitude and a vibrational feeling and sense of love, of interconnectedness, then you're more elevated in consciousness. From that elevated position, your intuition, gnosis, and understanding are much more immediate and clear. Thus, you can receive what is being offered—whether it is from us, other galactic civilizations, spiritual contacts, or from another human—with discernment and interpretation of the highest level.

Virginia: You have another statement, "Nothing is binding or absolute in the relative Universe in which you live." Could you clarify whether there are absolutes outside or beyond the relative Universe? And what you mean by relative Universe?

Hathors: The absolute is actually imbedded in and interpenetrates, or permeates, the relative Universe. It holds the relative Universe but paradoxically has no one location of its own, because it is in all locations at the same time. It is in the quantum field, to use the language of the sciences you now employ.

The relative Universe is everything that you know through your senses, because everything that happens is in relationship to something else. Nothing is truly independent. Everything is interrelated. For instance, if the trees and plants on this planet were to decide to go on strike and not produce oxygen, the human species and its many civilizations would not last very long. They would disappear. Life as you know it would be gone. So man, who arrogantly considers himself to be the pinnacle of nature, could actually be eliminated by the plant world if the plants were not to participate. Everything is interconnected. We are interrelated. Even other dimensions are interrelated. That is why what is happening on planet Earth is so crucial and important, and why observers are coming from other realms to follow the outcome. They come because what is happening on this planet right now has reverberations interdimensionally and will affect other universes. So all things are really interconnected.

Virginia: How could what we do on Earth affect other universes?

Hathors: The ascension of a planet, which is basically what is happening in this situation, has tremendous repercussions because the octave shifts. It's as if you were listening to someone play the piano in the middle range of the keyboard. Then all of a sudden they go one octave higher, whereupon the music changes radically and everything in relationship to it will also change. That is what is happening here.

As Earth transits to a higher dimension, a higher frequency, everything in relationship to Earth–and that includes all the organisms, not just humans–is affected. Your solar system is affected, and through the law of resonance, the rest of the Universe–and even other dimensions–are affected. So it is a very positive thing that is getting ready to happen, and it has much interest for those who understand the process and for those who have the means to get here to observe.

Virginia: How do they get here to observe?

Hathors: Interesting phenomena. Some of them make a shift in awareness and are able to fold time and space and actually send a part of their awareness to be present here, although they are not here physically. Other cultures and civilizations have discovered how to transport themselves by what you might call astral traveling, and they are here in the subtler realms, very physically present but still in the subtle realms. Of course there are some other civilizations who have mastered the ability to transfer themselves physically, using what you would call a space ship, although that term is not really accurate in the way it is generally conceived. But it is a physical device. However, there are other even more esoteric ways, so you have a wide variety of means to get here to this quadrant of the Universe. Since the news has gone out that there is something significant happening on this arm of the Milky Way Galaxy, much activity abounds.

Virginia: In terms of the processes these beings use to be here, for whatever reason, are there dangers inherent for the human population in discerning who's who and what's what? How does a human being know who is friendly? If someone were to appear in a physical way–such as what we call a UFO–how can they protect themselves energetically when meeting such beings?

Hathors: Well, the energetics of this are extremely complex because when you have a being who has physically emerged into the third-dimensional reality from another dimension, with or without a device–as opposed to just having their awareness here–you have a different vibratory field from your own. Depending on the dimensions that they came from, their intentions and so forth, it gets very complex.

We therefore come back to this one piece of advice and not because we are trying to simplify something that is extremely complex. We advise it because it is the best means of protection and because it is also the best means of elevating one's destiny. Our advice is "to love," because love is the highest vibration, the fundamental octave, the fundamental tone that resonates throughout the entire

Universe and through all dimensions. This tone is the fabric that holds the worlds and atoms together. It holds and binds the interconnectedness of all things.

This fundamental tone, this fundamental vibration, if you were to enter it, becomes impenetrable, becomes invincible, and you cannot be harmed by any occurrence! This vibratory field of love is like being enclosed in a field of light whose purity cannot be assaulted. We are not talking about love as most humans conceive it to be, but as a total vibration that is so powerful it resonates through all the subtle bodies and actually sets up a harmonic resonance. Within that loving harmonic resonance you are shielded, if you wish to use that term–although that is not quite accurate–because there is nothing to protect yourself from when you are in that love state. In that true, deep vibration, you could meet any being from any quadrant, from the known or unknown Universe, and be safe. So that is the goal for protecting oneself when meeting extraterrestrials–but it is far more important than this one application.

Virginia: Thank you. Then are you saying that the people who were abducted and had experiences of E.T. negativity or difficulties, over these past decades, would not have been contacted if they had been in a state of love?

Hathors: The answer is not quite that simple. They might have been abducted but they would not have been harmed. They *could not* have been harmed. Again, we are not saying that those who were abducted and had implants and/or negative experiences did not have love. That is not what we are saying. In addition to possible *karma*, their harmonic was just not strong enough to protect them. The question is simply how strong is your harmonic vibration?

Virginia: Is that why groups that are together in meditation create this higher harmonic?

Hathors: Where two or more gather in love there is a third power that is more powerful than the two, as you have been taught.

Virginia: Regarding the many channelers today who are bringing forth information, have you any comments regarding the kind of discernment we should use in accepting information from beyond our own level of consciousness here?

Hathors: First of all, don't automatically assume that because the information is coming from a disincarnate being, one who is not embodied, that it is any wiser or has any more valuable information than what might be said to you by another human. Just because one does not have a body does not mean that one is wise. There are a lot of unconscious beings without bodies; and we have met many of them (...laughter...). But in terms of discernment we would say to use the two fundamental powers you have as a human. These are the power of the heart and the power of the mind, or what you call discernment.

Don't unquestioningly take what is said as truth. Filter it through your heart and see how it feels to you—sense if it is the truth. And after you filter it through your heart, use your logic and your capacity to reason, to fathom it. Don't receive things passively by just accepting that the information is truth. Thoughtfully examine the information; test its mettle to see if it holds up. And then test it in your life and see if it works. This applies to everything we say, too!

Virginia: Related to that, there have been some disincarnate beings who say that we should receive implants to help us ascend, and there is a current controversy about whether this is advisable. Do you wish to speak to that?

Hathors: To receive something within oneself that is not harmonically suited or part of one's being is not only superfluous but it is possibly dangerous. You have within your being everything that is needed to ascend the spiral into the highest elevated states of consciousness. They are all within you in a seed form.

There is nothing that needs to be added from outside. All that needs to be done is to cultivate the soil of your being so that the seeds can emerge and give fruit. This is done through love, compassion, discernment or reason.

Virginia: Thank you. One of the things that is confusing to us humans down here is all the conversation about the various realms, domains and dimensions of consciousness which exist simultaneously. How can we help ourselves understand, while being in a body, how all of this works? I know this is a huge question but it's very frustrating to many people.

Hathors: Our perspective is that consciousness expresses itself into and through matter–and that matter is then elevated by consciousness into life. That life becomes increasingly more complex and more elevated until finally you have a consciousness that can hold an awareness of self in relationship to nature. Then it holds a consciousness of relationship between itself and the force behind nature or within nature, and that is what you call God. For you, at this time, that step–the process of moving into these elevated states–occurs through having a human form. We do not see this as a curse. We do not see this as a punishment. We see this as a tremendous opportunity for the expansion of consciousness in a unique way, through the balancing of that which is timeless and formless with that which is bound in time and form. It is a unique dichotomy. The pressure between those two–the part of you which is timeless and that physical part of you in time–creates an alchemical flow of magnetism–and out of that flow consciousness is elevated.

Virginia: I remember you saying, earlier, that the Hathors came from another Universe. In terms of what you just explained, how is that possible?

Hathors: Your three-dimensional Universe is only one of many universes. Our origins are what might be termed "non-physical" in that our Universe is primarily one of energy, light and sound. In our Universe of origin, matter, as you experience it here in the third-dimensional world, is basically non-existent. The "particles" that make up our world are extremely ephemeral by your standards. There is even less solidity in our Universe than in yours, and your world is about *99 percent* space!

This statement may seem odd to some, but universes are laid out in geometric configurations. From the perspective of hyperspace, it is as if each universe is confined within a kind of sphere or donut-like shape. These are laid out in rows or spirals, and it is possible to "pop" in and out of these different universes if one knows how.

Your body can be located in three-dimensional space by identifying coordinates that place you somewhere on Earth's surface (longitude and latitude). Earth, in turn, can be located in three-dimensional space in relation to the sun and other planets. It is also located in a specific region on the spiral arm of your Milky Way Galaxy. This is only one galaxy among thousands within your Universe, and each of these galaxies has a three-dimensional spatial relationship to all other galaxies. In your three-dimensional Universe, then, spatial location is crucial for determining where something or someone is located.

This is not true of non-physical hyperspace. *Location in non-physical realms is not done spatially but through a refined attribute of consciousness that is a combination of both thought and feeling.* In other words, if we want to make contact with someone we do not need any spatial coordinates. We hold that person "in thought" and feel or sense ourselves in their presence. Through the laws of harmonic resonance an aspect of our consciousness will "find" them. You have this ability as well. It is merely a question of developing it.

In regards to the interface between your Universe and ours, we know of only two pathways. One can enter your three-dimensional world from non-physical hyperspace, through a "portal" such as Sirius, or through the substratum of matter itself. If you enter into the substratum of time, space and matter you will make contact with an aspect of consciousness that is both omnipresent, meaning everywhere at once, and multi-dimensional, meaning expanded through all dimensions, not just the third. This process of making contact with the substratum of your Universe or what your physicists call the quantum field, is done through the agency of consciousness itself. If one knows how, one can enter in and go out of this world through "micro-portals" that hover around sub-atomic particles. This is not the pathway we used, however, to enter your Universe. With a few exceptions, we entered your physical Universe through the galactic portal of Sirius.

Virginia: Some of our outstanding physicists believe that the Universe is holographic. Is this your understanding?

Hathors: Yes, that is our view. Your science of holography is still in its infancy, and you have, as the saying goes, "only scratched the surface." From our perspective, matter and energy are interchangeable, as your science has verified. Specifically, however, all matter is essentially "trapped light" or light lowered to a slower vibration. Holography has shown that you can create a three-dimensional image by photographing an image in a specific manner using a highly coherent beam of light called a laser. When you view the developed image in the same angle as it was photographed, you get the appearance of three-dimensionality.

We would like to suggest to you that this is exactly what happens to you every moment of your life. The physical world that you experience so substantially is a mirage created by the holographic nature of matter. Your consciousness is literally like a laser beam of coherent light. All that has happened here, is that, as humans, you have agreed how to hold the lens of your consciousness so that you all "see" the same thing. However, you are not neurologically bound to this appearance of things. By changing how you hold the focus of consciousness, you can change how you perceive the world. This is not done through thought as you normally think of it, however. It is accomplished through a powerful alignment of awareness and intention. The two of these together can literally "warp" the fabric of space and time and present a very different world to be perceived.

Your experience of both yourself and your world is created, fundamentally by you, at the deepest levels of consciousness. At this profound level where mind and matter meet, the holographic nature of matter is expressed through your brain and nervous system. Thus, you experience the world as an "objective," "external," and "substantial" three-dimensional reality. In fact, your reality is anything but objective, external, substantial or three-dimensional. These illusions are created and sustained by how you hold the focus of your awareness. This is a learned process that was taught to you (unconsciously for the most part) by your parents, teachers and peers. As a learned habit of perception, it can be altered. This alteration of perception is crucial if you desire to directly experience what we are talking about. In this regard, you will find the exercises that we have given most helpful in that they gently train your nervous system to perceive this "hidden reality."

As your science has verified, holograms have the unique quality of embedding information. For instance, if you take a hologram and cut the image into several pieces, each of those pieces will hold the entire image in minuscule, no matter how small you make the pieces. In holograms, the whole is held within the part. Since the entire Universe is holographic in nature, and you are a part of it, you hold access to the entire holographic reality of your Universe within your own body. And we might add, you have access to non-physical dimensions as well.

Virginia: That's very lovely. Thank you. This brings

me to my last question about "living life in service to life."
Please give us some healthy and practical ways to put
"living life in service to life" into everyday practice.

Hathors: Every interaction you have with another
human being is an opportunity to serve life. When you
stop to fill your car with gas, when you go to the grocery
store, or when you see a fellow worker, it's an opportunity
to be kind and concerned. If you are so rushed or so involved with your own affairs, however, that other people
are merely objects, then you have missed one *new* moment of sacredness. You have missed an opportunity to
serve life. But when you are in these situations and you
pause for just a moment, remembering that you are with
another human sharing the Sacred Mystery of life, you
have the opportunity to serve life.

Indeed, if you pause and look another in the eye, or
you simply acknowledge them in some way for being something more than an object, then you have served life. So
every relationship is an opportunity. It's not just how much
you say or do; it's an attitude that is held within your
energy field. Simply hold the attitude that all persons you
meet–whether you like them or not–are part of the great
Universe, because that is an accurate description. Indeed,
if you truly hold that belief, that remembrance in yourself, then you are making something sacred or holy.

The true meaning of holy goes back to the concept of
wholeness, to make whole. So to make whole is to do holy
work–the sacred task of unifying the great Universe in
awareness. This is done from human to human or sometimes human to pets, animals, plants and other life-forms.
Essentially it's done from being to being. By acknowledging within yourself that each being you meet has value,
you serve life. You may not know who they are, their history, or what they believe, but they are part of life and so
you acknowledge them. If you hold that intent in your
energy field, love and acceptance get communicated to
them. And that is serving life.

Virginia: Beautiful. What a fine way to end a book. Do you have any final statement you would like to add?

Hathors: We would say in final closing that within you, the human, is a great mystery waiting to unfold itself and to bedazzle you. All that is needed is the touch of love. So love yourself, love others. It is that simple. So be it through all time and all space.

We are your spiritual companions,

The Hathors

LIST OF SELF-MASTERY EXERCISES
AND DIAGRAMS

continued on page 226 . . .

LIST OF SELF-MASTERY EXERCISES
AND DIAGRAMS Continued ...

Did you know that the entire human race can be raised into a mass ascension experience? ...that photon energy could be used to raise our consciousness?... that alchemy may be closer than you think? What was the effect on our planet Earth of the comets' collision with Jupiter? Learn more about the true nature of time.

New Teachings for an Awakening Humanity, 1994/95 Revised Edition.

Here's an extraordinary book that has been highly recommended by Judith Skutch, A Course in Miracles; Eileen Caddy, Findhorn Community; and John Randolph Price, author. You will learn more about the true reason for Jesus' mission 2000 years ago and at the same time see a glimpse of the wondrous future that awaits us on earth. "I come to advise you that humanity is not alone in the Universe...that your Earth is now being raised back into the higher love dimension she once held." – *The Christ*. The original text has been updated with over 50 pages of new information including two additional chapters titled the "Alchemy of Ascension" and "Your Natural Inheritance Reclaimed." *Virginia Essene, Editor.*

Spiritual Education Endeavors Publishing Company
1556 Halford Avenue #288, Santa Clara, CA 95051-2661 USA
(408) 245-5457

$9.95 paperback • 5.5 X 8.5 •264 pages • ISBN 0-937147-09-5
Library of Congress Catalog Card Number 94-068706

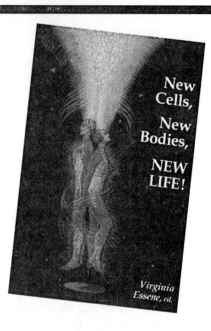

"Having trouble separating your delta waves from your thetas and super high Betas? Fear not: Tom Kenyon will help you get a grip on your consciousness, sub-consciousness, and altered consciousness in his book."

BRAIN STATES

TOM KENYON, M.A.

300 Pages • $11.95 Retail • ISBN 1-880698-04-9

Brain States, Kenyon, a psychologist and a musician, has spent years studying the effects of sound, music, and language on the human nervous system. Kenyon offers a technical excursion into how the brain works, noting the clear distinction between brain and mind. To do this he ascends to the heavens with Pegasus and drops by a shopping mall puddle to visit an amoeba. Through Kenyon's book, you will learn to overcome test anxiety, increase your intelligence, power your athletic abilities, hone your language skills, cure numerous psychological problems, tweak your creativity, and jump into altered states of consciousness.

UNITED STATES
PUBLISHING

AVAILABLE THROUGH: S.E.E. PUBLISHING

The Hathors' Self-Mastery Exercises on Audio Tape

The Self-Mastery Exercises in this book are also available on a convenient audio cassette tape. The tape was recorded by channel Tom Kenyon.

On this tape, Tom uses his remarkable four-octave vocal range, accompanied by the Tibetan bowl, to call the names of the archangels. This extraordinary sound called "toning" lifts one's subtle bodies into a high frequency state as a prelude to doing one or more of the Self-Mastery Exercises.

Tom guides the listener through each exercise and incorporates background psychoacoustic sound tracks to facilitate integration of the exercises. A special heart-opening meditation with the Hathors is also included!

Single cassette T102 $9.95. Order form is on the last page.

Tom Kenyon's ABR Audio Products

In 1983 Tom Kenyon, M.A., formed Acoustic Brain Research (ABR) to scientifically document the effects of sound and music on human consciousness. As a psychological counselor and musician, Tom discovered that sound and music could be powerful catalysts for both personal growth and healing. By enrolling the efforts of numerous researchers in both private and university settings, ABR has substantially documented the positive benefits of psychoacoustic technology.

S.E.E. Publishing Company is now (as of November 1997) distributing all of Tom's ABR tapes and compact discs. S.E.E. also sells Tom's book *Brain States*.

ABR tapes are remarkably successful in helping you achieve the self-enrichment and self-empowerment goals you seek. This is because of the scientific research, creative artistry, and advanced technology ABR invests in each program.

Music and sound have, from man's earliest cultures, been known to influence our states of mind. Now, through the application of advanced engineering, ABR utilizes the physics and psychology of sound to bring new scientific meaning and direction to this wondrous phenomenon.

ABR technology uses a variety of natural and electronic sounds, including specific sound patterns and frequencies, differentiations of tone and vibration, synchronization, oscillations

Spiritual Education Endeavors Publishing Company
1556 Halford Avenue #288, Santa Clara, CA 95051-2661 USA
(408) 245-5457

and pulsations, verbal and non-verbal input, tonal architecture, and hemispheric spanning. These are all orchestrated to stimulate the brain/mind into more resourceful states of awareness. Today, ABR is a recognized leader in psychoacoustic development and is acknowledged by professionals and lay persons alike as a source of the most advanced and neurologically-sound audio tapes available today.

If you would like to get on Tom Kenyon's mailing list in order to be notified about his **seminars and workshops**, please write to him at: P.O. Box 1148, Eastsound, WA 98245.

BioPulse Technology™

ABR psychoacoustic technology is based on the use of complex tonal matrices in which various sound patterns are mixed to stimulate the brain/mind into more resourceful states. Many of these tones are mixed beneath the level of audible hearing, masked by other sounds, or sometimes music, specifically composed for the desired mental/emotional state.

ABR tapes and CD's also take advantage of "biopulse technology™" in which specific tones, known to affect brain states, are mixed into the tonal matrix. Research indicates that such frequencies can significantly alter awareness. These biopulse frequencies fall into a few broad categories, and a parenthetical note after each tape title/description indicates which biopulse frequencies are used.

The primary categories of the biopulse frequencies are:

Delta (0.5-4 Hz) - associated with deep levels of relaxation such as sleep

Theta (4-8 Hz) - associated with tranquil states of awareness in which vivid internal imagery can often occur

Alpha (8-12 Hz) - relaxed nervous system, ideal for stress management, accelerated learning, and mental imagery

Beta (12-30 Hz) - associated with waking/alert states of awareness

K-Complex (30-35 Hz) - clarity and sudden states of integration, the "ah-ha" experience

Super High Beta (35-150 Hz) - psychodynamic states of awareness

AUDIO PRODUCT DESCRIPTIONS

Relaxation and Stress Management

Sound Bath
Soothe and relax yourself with this wonderful mix of beautiful music and ambient nature sounds. One of our most popular tapes for relaxation. (Theta range)
Single cassette T209 $13.95, compact disc CD209 $17.95

Wave Form
Wave Form gently "massages" your brain, helping you to dissolve tensions and drift into deeply relaxing states of awareness. (Theta range)
Single cassette T202 $13.95 *Headphones suggested.*

Wave Form II
Based on an ancient mantra believed to be the sound of the inner heart, this tonal matrix gently "opens the heart" thereby raising consciousness to a purer state of awareness, self-awareness and harmony. Beautiful vocals are intertwined with deep harmonic musical passages. (Theta range)
Single cassette T203 $13.95 *Headphones suggested.*

Rest and Relaxation (R & R)
For busy people who don't always get the rest they need, this tape includes *The 24-Minute Nap* and *The 22-Minute Vacation*. People love this tape! (Mid-Alpha to low Delta range)
Single cassette T206 $13.95 *Headphones suggested.*

Homage to Sol
Beautiful repetitive tempos for guitar, flute, and cello. Based on discoveries of the Lozamov Institute, this beautiful and restful music opens new vistas of serenity.
Single cassette T201 $13.95

Meditation

The Ghandarva Experience
A powerful journey into the spiritual realms of being. This unique program includes a 30-minute talk on the history of the Ghandarva and traces its roots back to Vedic India. Part Two is a compelling listening experience and includes the Chant of the Archangels and the Calling of Sacred Names, the Ghandarvic Choir, and a beautiful rendition of the 23rd Psalm.
Single cassette T801 $17.95, compact disc CD801 $19.95

Singing Crystal Bowls

Ethereal sounds of quartz "singing crystal bowls" to enhance altered states of awareness. Stimulate your body's energy centers as you allow these evocative "crystal vibrations" to flow throughout your body.
Single cassette T203 $13.95

> Other titles that can also be used for meditation:
> Sound Bath T209 or CD 209
> Wave Form T202
> Wave Form II T203
> Creative Imaging T205
> The Hathors' Self-Mastery Exercises T102

Fitness

The Zone

A delightful and truly effective tape designed to be used with a "Walkman-type" cassette player while doing aerobic exercises such as running, walking, using a treadmill, etc. Increases your self-motivation and encourages a more intense workout. (Alpha-Beta)
Single cassette tape T605 $13.95 *Headphones suggested.*

Self-Healing and Recovery

Psycho-Immunology

This widely acclaimed "self-healing" program helps you to explore the body/mind connection. It has been created to help you develop a greater potential for "healing experiences," and to assist you in your natural self-healing abilities. Note: Not a substitute for medical treatment. (Alpha-Delta)
Set of 3 tapes T401 $49.95 *Headphones suggested.*

Yoga for the Eyes

This tape offers eye movement exercises, guided imagery, and musical patterns to help rejuvenate your physically-strained and stress-weary sight. (Mid-Alpha range)
Single cassette tape T608 $13.95 *Stereo headphones required.*

Freedom To Be

Free yourself to make healthier decisions and live a fuller life. Designed as a recovery program for alcoholism and drug addiction, these tapes have been found to be very helpful with issues of low self-esteem, self-sabotage, and emotional

overwhelm. (Theta) *Headphones suggested.*
Two tape set with instructions T602 $29.95

Transformation Now!
A highly intense psychoacoustic stimulation of the brain/mind for rapid personal transformation. Note: Epileptics and persons with brain damage should not listen to this tape without professional supervision. (Shifts rapidly through Alpha, Theta, and Delta)
Single cassette tape T303 $13.95 *Headphones suggested.*

Healing the Child Within
Unique guided imagery helps you to resolve deeply-held childhood issues. (Alpha to Theta range)
Single cassette tape T601 $13.95 *Headphones suggested.*

Mind/Brain Performance Increase

Creative Imaging
Processes used with this tape have been documented in independent tests to significantly improve analytical abilities, creative problem solving, learning, and insight. Protocols accompanying the tape can also be used to increase visualization abilities. (Mid-Alpha)
Single cassette T205 $13.95 *Headphones suggested.*

Mind Gymnastiks
This "flagship" of ABR's programs has been hailed by researchers, professionals, and laypersons as a highly innovative and powerful tool for helping to increase mental abilities and performance. Users report expanded creativity, speed of processing, perceptual clarity, and feelings of "being on top of things." (Low Delta to K-complex) *Stereo headphones required.*
Set of 6 tapes with instructions T700 $99.95

Inspired: High Genius and Creativity
Utilizing visual imagery and sophisticated archetypal psychology, these participatory tapes help you tap into the creative principles that great scientists and artists have used throughout history. Enter meditative states where enhanced visualization and inspired dreams help you gain insights into problem solving and goal attainment. (Mid-Alpha range)
Headphones suggested.
Set of 4 cassette tapes with manual T701 $89.95

LOVE CORPS NETWORKING

The term *Love Corps* was coined in the book *New Teachings for an Awakening Humanity*. The Love Corps is a universal alliance of all human beings of good will who seek both inner personal peace and its planetary application. Thus the worldwide Love Corps family is committed to achieving inner peace through meditation and self-healing and to sharing that peace in groups where the unity of cooperation can be applied toward the preservation of all life.

In order to support our lightworkers, wherever they may be, we publish the Love Corps Newsletter. Its purpose is to keep our Love Corps family informed of the very latest information being received from the Spiritual Hierarchy. Newsletter subscribers are eligible to join the Love Corps Network "Hot Line." Please send a SASE for an application.

Virginia Essene frequently travels around the United States and the world to link Love Corps energies, to share additional information not included in the books *The Hathor Material: Messages from an Ascended Civilization; You Are Becoming a Galactic Human; New Cells, New Bodies, New Life!; New Teachings for an Awakening Humanity; Secret Truths: A Young Adult's Guide for Creating Peace; Cosmic Revelation; and Descent of the Dove*, and to encourage humanity's achievement of peace and the preservation of all life upon planet earth.

Please contact us for further information if you would like to be involved in the Love Corps endeavors or to participate with us in seminars. Also contact us to schedule a soul reading or an individual counseling session, in person or by telephone.

This "Time of Awakening" brings a new spiral of information to move each of us to a higher level of inner peace and planetary involvement. You are encouraged to accept the responsibility of this evolutionary opportunity and immediately unite efforts with other people in creating peaceful attitudes and conditions on our planet.

SHARE FOUNDATION
1556 Halford Ave. #288
Santa Clara, CA 95051-2661 USA
Tel. (408) 245-5457   FAX (408) 245-5460
E-mail: lovecorp@ix.netcom.com

ORDER FORM

To: **S.E.E. PUBLISHING COMPANY**
c/o The SHARE FOUNDATION*
1556 Halford Avenue #288
Santa Clara, CA 95051-2661 U.S.A.
Telephone (408) 245-5457   FAX (408) 245-5460
E-mail: lovecorp@ix.netcom.com

AUDIO and VIDEO PRODUCTS
(T = tape, CD = compact disc, V = video)

Title	Code	Price	Qty	Title	Code	Price	Qty
Creative Imag.	T205	$13.95	___	Rest & Relax.	T206	$13.95	___
Freedom to Be	T602	$29.95	___	Singing C.B.	T203	$13.95	___
Ghandarva E.	T801	$17.95	___	Sound Bath	T209	$13.95	___
Healing . . .	T601	$13.95	___	The Zone	T605	$13.95	___
Homage to S.	T201	$13.95	___	Trans. Now!	T303	$13.95	___
Inspired: . . .	T701	$89.95	___	Wave Form	T202	$13.95	___
Mind Gymn.	T700	$99.95	___	Wave Form II	T203	$13.95	___
Psycho-Imm.	T401	$49.95	___	Yoga . . . Eyes	T608	$13.95	___

Hathors' Self-Mastery Exercises tape.......	T102	$ 9.95	___
Ghandarva Experience	CD801	$19.95	___
Sound Bath	CD209	$17.95	___
Sound Healing in the Inner Terrain of Consciousness with Tom Kenyon video	V101	$29.95	___

Total of audio tapes, CD's, and videos $_____
(Please enter total on other side of this page)

U.S. Shipping & Handling Charges

Product total $	Amount	Product total $	Amount
$00.00 - $14.99	$3.95	$45.00 - $59.99	$8.45
$15.00 - $29.99	$5.45	$60.00 - $74.99	$9.95
$30.00 - $44.99	$6.95	$75.00 - $99.99	$11.45
		$100.00 and up	$12.95

Notes:

• Canada & Mexico add $2.00 to above <u>amounts</u>.

• Other International charges vary by country and weight; please call, FAX, or e-mail for rates.

• Please send check or money order in **U.S. funds** payable through a U.S. bank, or send an International money order made payable to S.E.E. Publishing Co. We **do not accept** credit cards, foreign currency, or checks drawn on a foreign bank.

• We will ship your order by the best carrier. Some carriers do not deliver to P.O. boxes, so we must have both your street and postal address. **See next page to order books and newsletter. ⟶**

Order Form continued . . . BOOKS (U.S. $)

The Hathor Material .... @ $12.95 $_____

New Cells, New Bodies, NEW LIFE! .... @ $11.95 $_____

New Teachings for an Awakening Humanity:
English ed. **(Revised 1994/1995)**................ @ $9.95 $_____
Spanish ed. **Nuevas Ensenanzas**............. @ $5.95 $_____
or (Spanish only) 2 books for $10.00.................. $_____

Brain States by Tom Kenyon .... @ $11.95 $_____

Minus quantity discount (above items only)* .... $(_____)

Tapes, CD's, & Videos from other side .... $_____

Product total (above items)........... $_____

Plus 8.25% **sales tax** (California residents only) .... $_____

Plus **shipping & handling** (see other side):** ...... $_____
(Amount is based on **Product total**, above)

Please send me the **Love Corps Newsletter**:
☐ One year (bi-monthly) subscription = $24.................. $_____
☐ Canadian & other international = $30 (airmail) .... $_____
☐ Earlier issues @ $4/issue U.S.A., $5 foreign. Specify
year & mo. _____ J/F, M/A, M/J, J/A, S/O, N/D ...... $_____

Love Corps donation (tax deductible)*** .... $_____

TOTAL ENCLOSED (add items within box) .... $_____

Please PRINT (this information is for your mailing label)

_____
Name

_____
Address

_____
City   State/Province   Zip Code
(_____)_____
Area Code   Telephone Number (optional)

---

* Quantity discounts; books only:
5 to 9 books - take off 10%
10 or more books - take off 20%
** Please request shipping rates for first class or air mail.

*** The Share Foundation is a non-profit organization. Contributions are tax deductible under section 501(c)(3) of the IRS code.

All prices and shipping & handling charges are subject to change.